Ess

Sydney

by

ANNE MATTHEWS

Born in Cornwall, Anne Matthews is now
an adopted Sydneysider. She has put her
knowledge and love of the city to good
use, writing regularly about Sydney
in books and magazines.

Produced by the Publishing Division of
The Automobile Association

Written by Anne Matthews
Peace and Quiet section by Paul Sterry
Consultant: Frank Dawes

Edited, designed and produced by the Publishing Division of The Automobile Association. Maps © The Automobile Association 1990.

Distributed in the United Kingdom by the Publishing Division of The Automobile Association, Fanum House, Basingstoke, Hampshire, RG21 2EA

The contents of this publication are believed correct at the time of printing. Nevertheless, the publishers cannot accept responsibility for errors or omissions, nor for changes in details given.

A CIP catalogue record for this book is available from the British Library.

ISBN 0 86145 877 X

Published by The Automobile Association

Typesetting: Microset Graphics Ltd, Basingstoke
Colour separation: Mullis Morgan Ltd, London
Printing: Printers S.R.L., Trento, Italy

Front cover picture: Sydney Opera House

This book employs a
simple rating system to
help choose which
places to visit:

◆◆◆ do not miss

◆◆   see if you can

◆   worth seeing if
you have time

Australia's oldest and largest city and its economic and financial centre, Sydney is also a vibrant and exciting place picturesquely sited on Port Jackson, 'the finest harbour in the world'

INTRODUCTION

Far away from the old, crowded cities of Europe and the frantic pace of Tokyo or New York, Sydney's freshness and vibrancy is like a breath of Pacific fresh air. On a sunny day the harbour sparkles like a vast liquid jewel and the entire city seems like an event waiting to happen — and happening it is! In its short 200-year life, Sydney has developed from the dumping ground for Britain's unwanted to one of the world's great cities, and it is constantly changing, growing and adapting. Sydney has been likened to a young adolescent: brash, undisciplined and definitely anti-authority, it is still growing — sometimes beyond its own control — and it still doesn't know what it wants to be when it grows up. Growing up, or at least upwards, is something that Sydney specialises in. Constant building, demolishing and rebuilding have created a city full of high-rise structures, construction sites and cranes, and anyone visiting today after ten years away would hardly recognise many parts of the city. Sydney is growing outwards too. The First Fleet's reluctant 1,300 or so convicts and military migrants have swelled in just 200 years to almost 4 million, a quarter of Australia's total population. The metropolitan area is huge — 670 square miles (1,735 sq. km) of red-roofed houses, streets, parkland, industrial sites and waterways — and it doesn't take a mathematician to work out that this is a great deal of space for a relatively small number of people. The feeling of space is one of Sydney's most appealing characteristics.

The climate is not bad either. The city is in the warm temperate climatic zone, which means warm to hot summers and mild winters, and even if it does rain quite frequently, it is still a very pleasant place to live. There are other natural attractions too. The city is surrounded by still relatively unspoilt bushland and 37 miles (60km) of coastline with excellent sandy beaches, and it has an incredible 148 miles (240km) of harbour foreshore.

Sydneysiders are proud of their city, and even its history. Whereas in the past many people were ashamed of their 'convict stain' origins, recent years have seen a sense of pride develop, especially among those whose ancestors can be traced back to the First Fleet. And there aren't many cities in the world where the locals remain excited about their environment. You only have to sit on a Manly-bound ferry as it makes its way across the harbour, or on a train crossing the Harbour Bridge, to realise that most of those people craning their necks for a better view are the businessman on his way to work, or the housewife on a shopping trip.

If the Sydneysider still finds his or her own city appealing, the visitor will enthuse even more. For long a destination only for those with relatives here, or for the rich with enough time and money for a round-the-world cruise, the past few years have seen an amazing boom in the tourist trade. Perhaps it is all a part of

Sydney's coming of age, and the accompanying confidence to advertise its attractions to the world, but the tourists are now arriving in their droves, cramming the hopelessly inadequate airport which was never designed to cope with this huge influx of overseas arrivals, and causing a rash of hotel and tourist-related building. It all came to a head during the 1988 Bicentenary year, when Sydney put on a show like no other, and drew many thousands of visitors.

Sydney deserves this long overdue influx, as the city has many attractions; from the natural beauty of its waterways, bush and beaches, to the unique history of its Rocks area, and even the glass, steel and concrete of the modern and lively city it is today. Whatever the visitor's taste, there is something for everyone, and you will find Sydneysiders a friendly but not intrusive lot who are only too happy to chat, give directions or hand out some advice, so adding to the city's charm.

BACKGROUND

History

For centuries man believed in the existence of

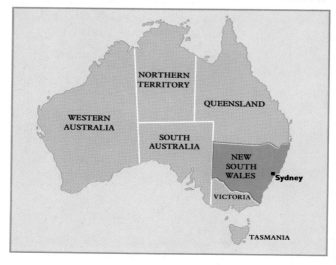

A contemporary painting shows Captain Cook taking possession of New South Wales for the British government in 1770. Behind him, the Endeavour lies at anchor in Botany Bay

a great southland with its accompanying riches of gold, spices and − in the face of religious zeal − souls to be saved. It was not until the early 17th century that Dutch sailors first sighted the north coast of Australia, but they saw little to arouse their interest, and this situation continued throughout the 17th century, as Dutch and English explorers touched on the north, west and southern coasts of the continent. It was not until 1770, when a Yorkshireman named James Cook was instructed to observe the transit of Venus at Tahiti, and continue the search for the southland, that the east coast of Australia was 'discovered', albeit by chance. Cook and his party, on the *Endeavour*, arrived in Botany Bay in April 1770 and spent several days here, observing the Aborigines and collecting flora and fauna specimens to take back to England. Cook noted that the land looked promising and that the natives were not interested in anything that was offered to them − as he wrote: 'all they seemed to want was for us to be gone'. Cook's party did not enter Sydney Harbour, but as they passed up the coast he noted a good anchorage, which he named Port Jackson, before continuing north and claiming this entire east coast of New Holland for King George III, naming it New South Wales.

Little was thought of this new English possession until Sir Joseph Banks, who had accompanied Cook on the 1770 voyage, suggested that it might be used as a penal colony. Until 1776 the British had used America for this purpose, but the rebellion there had ended this practice and by 1783 the overcrowded and rotting hulks on the River Thames were no longer suitable or adequate for the convict problem. Suddenly Banks' suggestion seemed like the answer to a prayer. By 1787, the colonisation plan had been put into action. Captain Arthur Phillip, a retired naval officer, was appointed Captain-General and Governor-in-Chief and instructed to found the intended Botany Bay settlement, cultivate the natives and explore and utilise the land. His charges consisted of 759 convicts, 191 of which were women, in a total of 1,350 men, women and children who were setting out, mostly against their will, to pioneer this new land. The First Fleet set sail from Portsmouth in May 1787, and travelling via Teneriffe, Rio de Janeiro and Cape Town, the 11 ships covered the vast distance in eight months. 14,000 miles (22,530km) away from home, the bewildered group arrived in Botany Bay on 20 January 1788 to the unpleasant sight of a barren and windswept scene which gave them little hope of Cook's vision of a fertile land suitable for cultivation. Their disappointment must have been heart-rending. However, Phillip sent a party north to enter Port Jackson, described by Phillip as 'the finest harbour in the world'. The colony was off and running.

The early days were terrible: the Sydney Cove soil was thin; poor food rations, compounded by the fact that supply ships from England did not arrive, led to near starvation and prevalent thieving, punishable by death; and severe conditions — floggings of up to 300 lashes were not uncommon for some offences — must have made many convicts wish that they had been hanged rather than transported. Slowly, things began to improve. Parramatta was founded in November 1788 as the centre of a fertile agricultural region, and the Windsor region for the same purpose in 1794. Convicts were assigned to soldier-farmers or free settlers and were granted pardons after a few years of good behaviour, but increasing corruption, drunkenness and lawlessness made the colony a treacherous place. All that improved greatly in 1810, on the arrival of Governor Lachlan Macquarie; by 1821 when he departed for England he had turned New South Wales into a real colony, and was later given the name 'father of Australia'.

Macquarie set about improving public morals, creating a proper town plan, encouraging convict emancipation and setting up a plan of public buildings, including those designed by Francis Greenway, which still adorn Sydney today. The colony also began to expand its horizons, spreading over the Blue Mountains in 1813 and south to Wollongong by 1815; these explorations discovered the vital farming land which would keep the fledgling colony alive and thriving. By 1818 trade in the form of wool and whale oil was established, and in 1819 the arrival of many free settlers, as well as the frequent shiploads of convicts, had boosted the population to over 26,000, just over a third of which were convicts.

By 1832 it seems that Sydney and New South Wales were not such bad places to be. The British government began an assisted emigration programme, with over 70,000 people arriving in Sydney over the next ten years, and in 1840 convict transportation

It seems that the unfortunate Australian natives were already bowing down to the white man as soon as Governor Phillip and the First Fleet landed in January 1788

ceased. The city's expansion continued — Sydney Cove was still the heartland, but suburbs such as Balmain and Paddington came into being — and in the 1850s the city and state's population was further swelled by the discovery of gold near Bathurst, on the other side of the Blue Mountains. This gold rush brought men and women of many nationalities — the Chinese in particular — to further diversify the already mixed bag of people. The scene was set for today's constant growth and multiculturalism.

Bare Island Fort, off shore in Botany Bay, was built in 1881. Although its guns have never been fired in anger, they are sometimes discharged now in celebration or on ceremonial occasions

Other landmarks followed: a period of growth and prosperity saw many of the city's grand buildings come into being; in 1888 the city celebrated its centenary with the establishment of Centennial Park; and in 1901 Federation brought the beginning of the Commonwealth of Australia. By 1925 the Sydney metropolitan area contained over one million people and in 1932

the Harbour Bridge was opened. The post-war era saw great waves of immigration as displaced persons from Europe added their cultures, food and lifestyles to an already diverse population, which by 1963 had topped the two million mark. The idea of sending a bunch of thieves and soldiers to the other side of the world was a bizarre one, but by some twist of fate it has worked, and worked splendidly.

The First Sydneysiders

Somewhere around 50,000 years ago, the Australian Aborigine arrived from the north and began the nomadic hunting and gathering life which continued, unhindered and uninterrupted, until the first real threat appeared over the horizon in 1770. James Cook, for all his good intentions and belief in the ideal of the 'noble savage', has a lot to answer for. He noted that the Aborigines of the Sydney region seemed content with their lot — the men hunted game, while the women foraged for fruits and small animals, and the fish were plentiful. In the outer Sydney region some evidence of this life remains in the form of rock carvings at Ku-ring-gai Chase National Park, while 1987 excavations near Richmond in the northwest of the area revealed stone tools which date back some 45,000 years.

In 1788 all that changed. Initially the natives wisely kept their distance from the white man, but the inevitable conflict began once they realised that these strangers were here to stay and that they were being displaced from their fishing, hunting and, even more importantly, their sacred grounds. Several attacks on the intruders followed, which brought out the muskets and the wrath of the white man. The effects of diseases such as smallpox, measles and influenza followed, as did the discovery of rum, which turned these once proud people into drunken, apathetic and poverty stricken fringe dwellers of European society. Within three years of the white man's arrival, the Aboriginal population of Sydney was reduced by two thirds, with further dramatic reductions occurring over the next 50 years. Today's small Aboriginal population lives mostly in run-down suburbs such as Redfern and La Perouse, and is a sad reminder of how one culture can thrive at the expense of another. The 1988 Bicentenary was, for most, a time to celebrate, but for Sydney's Aborigines it was an appropriate occasion for protest.

The City and its People

When the first settlers arrived in what was the newest and least known of the 'new worlds' they brought with them the ideas, thoughts and manners of the old country, and set about creating an isolated and remote pocket of England in this *terra incognito*. But the climate, environment and distance from home were all to affect these imported values. Slowly but surely the colony developed its own character: architecture changed to suit the climate, shady verandahs being added to combat the summer heat; and speech patterns altered. By the 1820s visitors from England noticed that the young people born in the colony (the 'currency') not only spoke differently, but also looked stronger and healthier than their English counterparts. As the colony progressed and more convicts were emancipated, inter-marriage between different classes became common, something which would have been unheard of back in the old country. Most of these changes were born of necessity, but they have persisted to make Sydney and Australia what they are today. Sydneysiders have always been a mixed bag of people: although most members of the first and subsequent fleets were of Anglo-Saxon extract, there was a large Irish contingent, and a significant proportion of British blacks. This multinationalism has continued so that today around 70 per cent of Sydneysiders are a combination of at least two different ethnic backgrounds. One wonders what the situation will be in another 100 years. Migration waves of Chinese, Lebanese, Germans, Greeks, Italians, Yugoslavs, Maltese, Turks, Jews and more recently Vietnamese and South Africans, have all added ethnic tinges in cultures, language, cuisine and behaviour to create a colourful polyglot of people. Perhaps it is too soon for the real impact of this multiculturalism to make itself felt on Sydney, but today the prevailing

The meandering foreshores of Sydney Harbour – one of the world's largest and most enchanting harbours – cover almost 150 miles (240km)

attitude and character of Sydneysiders is one of relaxed, casual, sometimes almost apathetic complacency. For many, Sydney is the best city in the world's best country, so we just sit back and enjoy that fact or fallacy; try not to work too hard; spend most of the working week looking forward to the weekend; and drink, eat and party far too much. Whatever the real reasons, Sydneysiders are laid-back and casual, generally very friendly and outgoing, but with a strong streak of anti-authoritarianism.
There is also a great deal of speculation that this is the land, and city, of opportunity and egalitarianism. It still is the former, but even though strict class barriers do not exist in the same way as in English society, there is a distinct, and growing, difference between rich and poor. You only have to visit a harbourside millionaire's suburb such as Point Piper or

Darling Point, and then trek out to the heavily
Vietnamese area of Cabramatta in the
southwest of the city to see this disparity. But
despite this, it is still a lot easier in Sydney to
meet and mingle with those of very different
backgrounds than it ever could be in the old
and staid societies of Europe.

And what of the city itself? Within this vast area
which has been spreading and sprawling for
200 years, there is a wide range of vistas, from
the always fascinating and attractive view of the
harbour from any angle, to the seediness of a
run-down suburb such as Redfern, or the
industrial landscape of Port Botany with its
docks and container terminals. Even though this
city is far more beautiful than most from its
good side, it still has the best-forgotten warts

Much of Sydney's big business is located in the area around Pitt and Bridge Streets: here you will find international airlines, multinational companies and state government buildings

which any large city spawns in its lifetime, but this is something which most visitors neither wish nor intend to see. Architecturally, there is also great diversity. Graceful Georgian buildings, such as Francis Greenway's Hyde Park Barracks, stand next to 1970s high-rise city monsters, while at least some of the newer city office blocks have made some attempt at attractiveness. In the suburbs, terraced houses with the classic Sydney iron lacework balconies and fences contrast with huge apartment blocks; and verandahed, gabled Federation-style houses stand beside ugly brick veneer dwellings from the post-war period. The face of this city is as varied as the people who live in it, and like everything else here, it is constantly shifting and changing. Despite certain annoyances like increasing air and water pollution, high house prices, terrible traffic snarls and the inevitable ocker element − the less desirable, loudmouth, often drunk Sydney hooligan − there is so much to recommend this city, as any visitor will discover, even if on a short visit. When the sun shines, as it often does, and you are out on the harbour, or sitting enjoying good food and fine wines at an outdoor restaurant, it seems that there is no place in the world as pleasant as this. Sydney may not be, as is often suggested, the 'best address on earth', but it sure comes close.

Sydney's Regions

Sydney's huge metropolitan area can be fairly conveniently divided up into districts, some of which will be of little interest to the visitor, while others are essentials on the tourist trail. The inner city area is quite distinctly divided into two by the presence of the Parramatta River and Port Jackson, and it is on the southern shores of Port Jackson that most of the city's early development took place. The dividing waterway, bridged by three structures − the Harbour, Gladesville and Ryde Bridges − creates for many Sydneysiders a feeling of 'us and them'.

City Centre. Sydney's commercial heart is the area where the visitor will spend most of his or her time. In addition to the major shopping and business streets, the Central Business District (CBD) holds many of the city's attractions: the Opera House, Harbour Bridge, historic Rocks area and major museums and galleries. In comparison with the vast size of the metropolitan area, the centre is small and easy to get around. Many of its narrow streets have their origin in the cart tracks which led from Sydney Cove to the city's early outposts — fine in the 19th century, but a nightmare for today's large population and heavy traffic flow.

Inner East. The inner eastern suburbs of Woolloomooloo, Darlinghurst, Kings Cross and Elizabeth Bay are full of history — old houses and apartment blocks, quaint streets, flights of steps and tree-lined avenues all give this area a great deal of character. Many visitors will get to know this region well, as most of the city's hotels, motels and guesthouses are located here. Kings Cross used to be the city's bohemian quarter, but it has degenerated into a Soho-like region of sex shows, strip joints,

An elevated section of railway winds its way through Woolloomooloo, an eastern suburb only a 15-minute walk from the city centre

prostitution and drugs. Nearby Paddington is full of interest — old houses, hilly streets and interesting shops, with a mostly young, often trendy population.

East. The eastern suburbs stretch from Watsons Bay in the north to Coogee in the south, and as far west as Surry Hills. On the harbour side, lovely suburbs like Double Bay, Rose Bay, Vaucluse and Watsons Bay contain expensive homes, parks, tree-lined streets and great views of the harbour, which extends right to South Head, one of the two walls of rock which guard Sydney Harbour. From South Head to Coogee, high sandstone cliffs are broken by bays which contain the beaches of Bondi and Bronte. On the inland side, pleasant suburbs such as Bellevue Hill, Woollahra and Randwick surround parkland, while Centennial Park takes up a large chunk of the region and is fringed by shopping areas like Bondi Junction, and streets in which only the wealthy can afford to live.

Inner West. West of the Harbour Bridge the scenery changes dramatically, as docks and working class suburbs take over from yacht marinas and multi-million-dollar mansions. Many of this region's suburbs have become gentrified, but there is still much that is distinctly rundown and undesirable. Balmain and Birchgrove are interesting for their quaint streets and weatherboard houses, while Glebe, near Sydney University, has some excellent restaurants and interesting shops. This area contains many ethnic group settlements, for example Italians at Leichhardt, Greeks and Aborigines at Redfern.

South. Southern Sydney begins somewhere around Newtown and Redfern, colourful working class suburbs, and includes the Airport, historic Botany Bay and the Kurnell peninsula, industrial areas, and the surf beaches of Maroubra and Cronulla. Further south, the Georges River area marks a return to 'nicer' suburbs and large homes with waterfrontage access, before the city peters out in the unspoilt natural bushland of the Royal National Park.

Lower North Shore. Over the bridge lies another and quite different world. North Sydney with its high-rise office blocks has sprung up as a harbourside twin to the main CBD, but will be of little interest to a visitor. On either side of this concrete jungle lie the interesting areas of McMahons Point and Kirribilli, while to the west the attractive middle class suburbs of Greenwich, Lane Cove, Ryde and the expensive Hunters Hill stretch away towards Parramatta. East of the Bridge there are more desirable areas such as Neutral Bay, Cremorne and Mosman, with harbour beaches and good outlook points, and then Middle Harbour with its Spit Bridge which leads on to the seaside town of Manly and North Head.

Northern Suburbs. The northern part of Sydney covers a vast area and extends right to the outer limits of the Hawkesbury River. In between is stockbroker belt, the leafy, quiet and almost rural suburbs of Lindfield, Frenchs Forest, St Ives and Wahroonga, which contrast with the beachside settlements of Dee Why, Mona Vale and Palm Beach. On the inland side of this peninsula lies Pittwater, the city's most beautiful waterway and a haven for yachties, and Ku-ring-gai Chase National Park with its natural bushland and recreation facilities.

Parramatta and the Western Suburbs. This is not the loveliest part of Sydney, as a drive along Parramatta Road will reveal, but for most Sydneysiders it is home. Sydney's urban sprawl has made Parramatta — once a completely separate town — the geographical heart of the metropolitan area, and the administrative, commercial and industrial centre for this large western region. Parramatta is Australia's second oldest settlement after Sydney itself, and is full of historic buildings which will interest the visitor.

The Far West. Beyond Parramatta, north and south blend into one huge district: the far west, which stretches to the foot of the Blue Mountains, some 42 miles (70km) from the city centre. Areas such as Richmond and Windsor were early settlements and are of historic interest, while in the southern part of the region the urban sprawl to Liverpool gives way to isolated housing estates and farmland which spread south to the old towns of Camden and Campbelltown, established to service the colony's early sheep farming districts.

WHAT TO SEE

The Sydney sightseer has a
great deal to choose from, both
in the inner city region and the
suburbs. Most of these are
easily accessible, and are all on
the Sydney Explorer bus route.
The section on the major City
Sights has been divided into
areas, for ease of discovery in
the field, and this is followed by
a section on Sydney's Historical
Suburbs. Most of the city's main
museums and galleries do not
charge entrance fees, which
will make them even more
appealing to the visitor.

*Circular Quay East. It is hard to
believe that this was the birthplace
of Australia as it is known today*

CITY SIGHTS

Any sightseeing tour should start
where the city, colony and
indeed, the entire country, had
its beginnings. Sydney's Central
Business District (CBD) is small
and this makes a walking tour of
the most interesting sites not only
practicable, but also the best way
of really seeing and getting to
know this lively and vibrant city.

The Circular Quay Area

The first thing that any visitor
should do is to head for Circular
Quay and the harbour, which is
where the city began 200 years
ago. This is the area that
contains some of Sydney's
best-known landmarks.
Both buses and trains run to
Circular Quay.

CITY SIGHTS

◆◆◆
CIRCULAR QUAY

Many visitors wonder why a square-shaped quay should be named 'Circular'. It was rounded once, but in 1837 the quay was built and squared off to form the city's main port. Now that too has changed, and the quay is the terminus for the city's many ferries which run to Manly, the North Shore, Watsons Bay and suburbs west of the Bridge; most harbour cruises also leave from this point. The quay is a hive of activity, especially during peak hours when commuters arrive and leave in droves. At other times the area is full of tourists, enjoying the harbour outlook and sitting at one of the very pleasant cafés which ring the quay. Circular Quay also has an upper level railway station, part of the city circle line, and some interesting shops, including the excellent Travel Bookshop. From the quay, a covered walkway leads east (to the right) to the Opera House and there are a couple of cafés with outdoor tables at which to sit and admire the view of the Harbour Bridge.

◆
CUSTOMS HOUSE

The area behind Circular Quay is one of the city's major bus interchanges, from which most eastern and western suburb buses begin their journeys. Among all the glass and concrete of modern high-rise buildings, the Customs House stands out. Begun in 1844 this sandstone building is the only Victorian construction left in the area, and it is close to the spot where the British flag was first raised by the new arrivals in 1788. The old Customs House is used as offices and is not open to the public.

◆◆◆
SYDNEY HARBOUR BRIDGE

Better known to Sydneysiders as the 'Coathanger', for obvious reasons, the Bridge was begun in 1923 and opened to the public in 1932. Before this time, ferries were the only means of crossing the harbour — impractical in the age of motor cars and the daily mass migration across the water. The bridge's eight road lanes, two train tracks, footpath and cycleway carry many thousands of people and vehicles each day. It is in the *Guinness Book of Records* as the

world's widest long span bridge; the main span is 1,650ft (502.9m) long and 160ft (48.8m) wide, while the top of the arch is 439ft (134m) above harbour water level. These days the bridge is experiencing bad traffic hold-ups and is no longer deemed adequate, and construction of a harbour tunnel, expected to be completed in 1992, is underway. The view from the pedestrian walkway (access via Cumberland Street in The Rocks) is excellent, and it is also possible to view the harbour from the southeast pylon; access also from Cumberland Street. *Open:* (southeast pylon) Saturday to Tuesday, 10.00-17.00hrs.

Sydney Harbour Bridge and the Opera House: the tourist symbols of the city

♦♦♦
SYDNEY OPERA HOUSE
Bennelong Point

In its time, Bennelong Point has been an island, the site of a fort, linked to the mainland by a bridge, and, after 1902, a tram depot. It is named after Bennelong, Governor Arthur Phillip's favourite Aborigine, who accompanied him on a trip to England in 1792 and was even presented to King George III. All of this history was swept away in 1957, when an international competition was announced to design an opera house for the city. Well over 200 submissions from 32 countries were considered, and the winner, Joern Utzon of Denmark, had designed the most unusual and technically difficult of all. The very brilliance of his design has always been a matter of great controversy, but the end result has left Sydney with what is considered by many to be one of the wonders of the modern world. Opened in 1973, the Opera House has five performance halls and is home to the Australian Opera and Australian Ballet, as well as being the symbolic centre of Australian cultural life. Thirty years on from its first conception, it is still a stunning and revolutionary building: the soaring, sail-like roofs contain over one million Swedish ceramic tiles, while the stone base and steps were inspired by Mexican Mayan and Aztec temples. It took over 1,200 workmen 14 years to complete the building. Guided tours of the interior are provided each day from 09.00-16.00hrs, and are

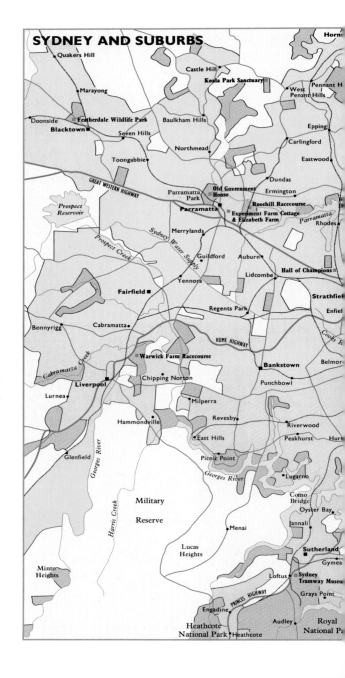

SYDNEY AND SUBURBS

Horns

Quakers Hill

Castle Hill
Koala Park Sanctuary

Marayong

West
Penant H

Pennant H

Doonside
Featherdale Wildlife Park
Blacktown

Baulkham Hills

Seven Hills

Epping

Carlingford

Northmead

Eastwood

Toongabbie

GREAT WESTERN HIGHWAY

Dundas
Ermington

Prospect
Reservoir

Parramatta
Park
Old Government
House
Rosehill Racecourse

Parramatta
Experiment Farm Cottage
& Elizabeth Farm

Parramatta

Rhodes

Prospect Creek

Merrylands

Sydney Water Supply

Guildford

Auburn

Lidcombe
Hall of Champions

Fairfield

Yennora

Regents Park

Strathfiel

Enfiel

Bonnyrigg

Cabramatta

Cooks R

Cabramatta Creek

HUME HIGHWAY

Bankstown

Belmor

Warwick Farm Racecourse

Chipping Norton

Punchbowl

Liverpool

Lurnea

Milperra

Revesby

Riverwood

Hammondville

East Hills

Peakhurst

Hurs

Glenfield

Georges River

Picnic Point

Georges River

Lugarno

Como
Bridge

Oyster Bay

Harris Creek

Military

Reserve

Menai

Jannali

Sutherland

Minto
Heights

Lucas
Heights

Loftus

Sydney
Tramway Museu

Gymea

Grays Point

Engadine

PRINCES HIGHWAY

Heathcote
National Park

Heathcote

Audley

Royal
National Pa

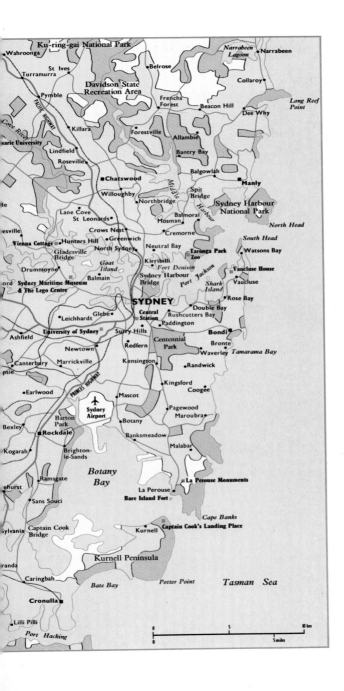

very worthwhile. The complex also houses the excellent Bennelong Restaurant, a shop and, at the northern end, an open-air cafeteria with free entertainment on Sunday afternoons.

Bus or train to Circular Quay

The Rocks

The promontory immediately to the west of Sydney Cove and Circular Quay is known as The Rocks and is the oldest part of Sydney, and indeed Australia.

The area got its name from the rocky sandstone slopes on which the first convict tents were erected in 1788. Gradually, this area became the focus of the new community, with the first fort, hospital, windmill and streets being built in The Rocks. The area became a violent and depraved seaport, full of illegal 'grog' shops and brothels, and by the 1850s an overcrowded and unhealthy slum — a situation which culminated in an outbreak of

*ne of the many pleasant places to
elax in the lovingly restored and
renovated area known as The Rocks*

interesting and historic area and
one in which the visitor should
spend as much time as possible.
The best way to approach The
Rocks is west from Circular
Quay towards George Street.

◆◆◆
CADMAN'S COTTAGE
110 George Street, The Rocks
Just behind the new overseas
passenger terminal and in
striking contrast is a small
sandstone cottage. Cadman's
Cottage is the city of Sydney's
oldest surviving house, built in
1816 as a barracks for the
Governor's boat crew, and
named after ex-convict John
Cadman, the government
coxswain who lived in the
simple building until 1854. The
cottage has been restored and
now contains the National Parks
and Wildlife Service information
centre and shop, which is full of
useful pamphlets and maps.
Open: Tuesday to Sunday, 10.00-
17.00hrs.
Train or bus to Circular Quay

◆◆
GARRISON CHURCH and
ARGYLE PLACE
Millers Point
Argyle Place is Sydney's oldest
village green and dates from
1830-50. Its somewhat run-down
buildings still exhibit fine
examples of the period's
architecture — note the
sandstone blocks and the iron
lacework used in the fences.
The Lord Nelson Hotel,
Sydney's oldest, with a licence
going back to 1844, is nearby.
The Garrison Church, or more
correctly, the Holy Trinity
Church, was completed in 1844
continued on page 28

bubonic plague in 1900. After
this, many of the old houses and
narrow lanes were destroyed,
while more were demolished
further up the hill in the 1920s to
make way for the Harbour
Bridge approach roads. The
Rocks has undergone a great
deal of restoration to turn it into
the tourist mecca it is now. It is,
however, still Sydney's most

continued on page 28

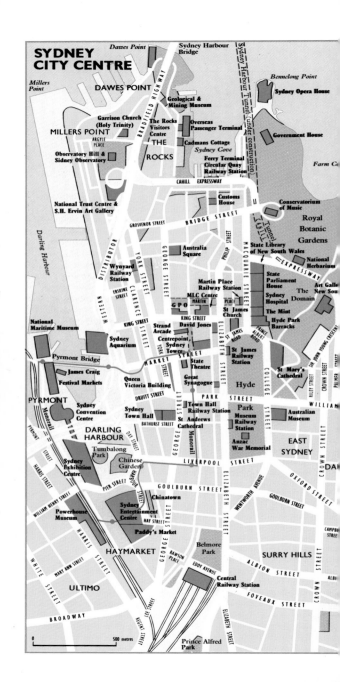

City Transport

Sydney's recently-opened, privately-owned Monorail, shown in red on the map, has provoked a strong reaction from Sydney's residents. Conservationists have been particularly angered by the design of the system's mirrored pylons; these, according to the objectors, make no concessions to their surroundings at all. The Monorail is, however, a convenient way to reach Darling Harbour, the revamped seaport area which now offers attractions such as a shopping centre, exhibition halls and recreational gardens.

The system operates from 08.00 to 22.00 (23.00 on Fridays and Saturdays); each train completes a loop every 12 minutes, and carries up to 500 people. The Monorail runs from the city centre past the Sydney Entertainment Centre and back across Darling Harbour, travelling over Pyrmont Bridge.

The city circle railway line runs via Central Station, Town Hall, Wynyard, Circular Quay, St James and Museum, with an additional city station at Martin Place.

and is a good example of the Gothic revival style. British Red Coats were stationed nearby from 1840-80 and used the church for prayer, hence the name which has continued to this day.
Bus 431 from George Street to Millers Point

◆◆
GEOLOGICAL AND MINING MUSEUM
36 George Street
A 1902 building with a tall chimney, built as an electric light station, houses an interesting Geological and Mining Museum, which is currently undergoing renovation and expansion. The museum features excellent collections of minerals, rocks and fossils, with an Australian emphasis. The days of the gold rush are commemorated by large gold nuggets, while there are also displays on the history of Australian mining and even a simulated underground mine. The shop sells a good selection of gemstones and minerals.
Open: Monday to Friday, 09.30-16.00hrs; Saturday 13.00-16.00hrs; Sunday 11.00-16.00hrs

◆◆
NATIONAL TRUST CENTRE and S H ERVIN GALLERY
Observatory Hill
The National Trust's New South Wales headquarters are housed in a building whose history goes back to 1815. Originally a military hospital built by Governor Macquarie, it became redundant when the barracks were moved to Paddington in the 1840s, and was used as a school from 1850 to 1974. Apart

from the excellent National Trust Australian theme book and gift shop, and the pleasant café, the complex includes the S H Ervin Gallery. This is one of Sydney's largest non-commercial art galleries, which, in addition to its large permanent collection, features informative changing exhibitions with an Australian history and environment theme.
Open: Bookshop: Monday to Friday 09.00-17.00hrs; Saturday and Sunday 14.00-17.00hrs. Gallery: Tuesday to Friday 11.00-17.00hrs; Saturday and Sunday 14.00-17.00hrs; admission charge.
Bus 431 from George Street to Millers Point

◆◆
OBSERVATORY HILL and SYDNEY OBSERVATORY
Millers Point
Originally known as Windmill Hill, this was the site of an early windmill, and later, an 1804 fort. At 144ft (44m), this is the city's highest natural point, and before the days of the Harbour Bridge and Opera House, was one of Sydney's most well-known landmarks. Today the hill is a park which features a rotunda, pleasant grassy lawns and a really good view of the harbour in three directions. The Sydney Observatory crowns the hill. Established in 1858 to study the little-known southern sky, the building incorporates a wall from the 1804 Fort Phillip, as well as the 1848 Signal Station, which was established here to send signals to ships in the harbour. By the 1970s increasing air pollution and the presence of

city lights made star-gazing impractical and the Observatory was converted into a museum of astronomy, which has many hands-on exhibits that children in particular will enjoy. For keen star-gazers, night-time observation sessions are conducted every night of the week, except Wednesdays. *Open:* Monday to Friday 14.00-17.00hrs; Saturday and Sunday 10.00-17.00hrs. For night sky viewing, call 241 2478 for bookings.
Bus 431 from George Street to Millers Point

◆
OVERSEAS PASSENGER TERMINAL
Circular Quay West
This is where the huge passenger ships such as the *QE2* dock while they are in Sydney, and the new building was completed in 1987 to replace an old structure. In addition to having three restaurants, the terminal affords a good view of the Opera House and Quay area.

Sydney Observatory, a charming colonial building of local sandstone

◆
ROCKS VISITORS CENTRE
104 George Street
From Cadman's Cottage, walk up the steps to George Street, which has many interesting buildings dating from 1838, to the Rocks Visitors Centre. Here you will find a great deal of information on The Rocks, as well as an invaluable pamphlet describing a walking tour of the area.

In addition to the specific sights mentioned above, visitors are reminded that the entire Rocks, Millers Point and Dawes Point area is a museum in itself; just walking around looking at streets such as **Argyle, Playfair** and **Lower Fort,** and buildings like the **Metcalfe Stores, Campbells Storehouse** and the terraced houses in **Upper George Street,** will take a full day. From The Rocks you can also visit **Pier One,** a shopping and restaurant complex on Walsh Bay, or walk onto the Bridge from Cumberland Street. There is much to see and do in the area.

Macquarie Street
Macquarie Street has long been the city's most stylish and exclusive avenue, and today it is one of the few areas which has retained its original atmosphere of Georgian elegance.
Originally (like all the city's main streets) a rough bush track heading south from Sydney Cove, it was remodelled by Governor Macquarie in 1810. Many of Macquarie Street's buildings are a tribute to the genius of Francis Greenway, a convict transported in 1813 for forgery, whose architectural skills transformed Sydney. Beginning from Circular Quay, you can walk the entire length of this interesting street, to Hyde Park and the city centre.

◆◆◆
HYDE PARK BARRACKS
Queens Square
This classic Georgian-style building is one of architect Francis Greenway's triumphs; he designed the three-storey, sandstone brick building in 1819 to house convicts, and it was later used, among other things, as a lodging house for destitute women. Extensive renovations from 1979 onwards have provided space for an excellent Museum of Applied Arts and Sciences outlet which gives an insight into the early days of the colony. Displays also feature the themes of immigration and how it has altered Sydney, and the city's big celebrations over the past 100 or so years. There is also a good museum shop which sells Australiana and books and, in the Barracks complex, an excellent restaurant.
Open: daily (except Tuesday) 10.00-17.00hrs; Tuesday 12.00-17.00hrs.

◆◆◆
THE MINT
Built in 1816, the Mint is one of the historic buildings in the attractive Queens Square area. Originally a section of the Rum Hospital, the building later became, after the 1851 gold rush, the first branch of the Royal Mint outside London, with gold coins in production from 1851 to 1927. The simple two-storey verandahed building

yde Park Barracks, originally built
house convicts doing public
orks, such as road-making, is now
ew South Wales' only museum of
ocial history

now a museum of Australian
olonial decorative arts and
cludes displays of coins,
amps and furniture.
pen: daily (except
Wednesday) 10.00-17.00hrs;
Wednesday 12.00-17.00hrs

◆◆
T JAMES' CHURCH
Queens Square
ydney's oldest church is
nother graceful Francis
reenway design, dating from
322. Built in the Colonial
eorgian style, this brick
hurch is now dwarfed by its
gh-rise neighbours, but the
324 spire was for many years
ne of the city's major
ndmarks. The stone porch was

added by John Verge, another
of Sydney's prominent early
architects, in 1832.
Open: Monday to Friday 08.00-
17.00hrs; Saturday 08.00-
18.00hrs; Sunday 08.00-16.00hrs

◆
STATE LIBRARY OF NSW
The State Library contains a vast
collection of books and
documents on Australia and the
Pacific region which are housed
in the 1910 Mitchell Wing at the
corner of Macquarie Street and
Shakespeare Place. Next door,
on Macquarie Street, the new
concrete and glass complex is a
striking contrast and houses
reference libraries, an excellent
bookshop and a gallery space
which holds changing exhibitions on Australian themes.
Open: Monday to Saturday
09.00-21.00hrs; Sunday 14.00-
18.00hrs

◆◆
STATE PARLIAMENT HOUSE
NSW has been governed from this simple but attractive colonial verandahed building since 1827. The building was once a wing of Governor Macquarie's Rum Hospital (so named because, in exchange for its erection, the builders were granted an extremely lucrative monopoly on importing rum into the colony). The structure dates from 1810-16, with several additions made in the 1840s. The building is open to the public for inspections, and it is also possible to sit in on evening sessions of Parliament. *Open:* Monday to Friday 10.00-15.00hrs. For evening sessions, book a seat by phoning 230 2111

◆
SYDNEY HOSPITAL
This Victorian sandstone complex was completed in 1894 and replaced the central block of the old Rum Hospital. Saved, after a long fight, from the developers' bulldozers in 1976, the hospital still thrives after almost 100 years of service.

All the Macquarie Street sights can be reached by taking a train to Martin Place station, then walking; they are also on the Sydney Explorer bus route

The Domain Area
Immediately behind Macquarie Street is the Domain, a 173 acre area of greenery, now divided into the Domain and the Royal Botanic Gardens by the Cahill Expressway. It was originally called the Governor's Domain and laid out in 1810 as part of Governor Macquarie's intention to create parkland.

◆◆◆
ART GALLERY OF NEW SOUTH WALES
Art Gallery Road
Housed in an imposing Victorian building which adjoins the Domain, the Art Gallery contains an extensive permanent collection of Australian art — ranging from Aboriginal paintings and artefacts to modern portraits and sculpture — as well as European and other art works. There is a good

As well as plants, the magnificently sited Botanic Gardens contain wide expanses of lawns and many fountains and statues

ollection of 19th-century
olonial art, including paintings
y Tom Roberts and Arthur
treeton. Special exhibitions,
/hich charge an entrance fee,
re held regularly and free
uided tours are available. The
allery has a good cafeteria
nd a shop selling books,
ostcards and gifts.
Open: Monday to Saturday 10.00-
7.00hrs; Sunday 12.00-17.00hrs.
*rain to Martin Place or St
ames; Free bus 666, or on the
ydney Explorer bus route*

◆◆
'HE DOMAIN
his park is in two parts. Behind
/lacquarie Street is a large

open space, ringed with lovely
old Moreton Bay fig trees, a
favourite haunt of joggers and
office workers at lunchtime, and
also the location for the Festival
of Sydney open-air opera and
classical music concerts each
January. On Sundays the Domain
becomes Sydney's version of
London's Speakers' Corner, with
orators of all persuasions putting
forth their ideas. The Art
Gallery is also in this area. The
second part of the Domain
continues past the Botanic
Gardens towards Mrs
Macquarie's Point. This is a
pleasant walk, and the view
from the Point takes in the
Opera House and Bridge, as
well as the lower north shore
and outer harbour. 'Mrs
Macquarie's Chair' is a seat
carved out of a large piece of
sandstone rock, with an
accompanying inscription. It is
also possible to reach Mrs
Macquarie's Point by walking
through the Botanic Gardens.

◆◆◆
ROYAL BOTANIC GARDENS
Mrs Macquarie's Road
Covering 74 acres of land which
hugs the crescent-shaped Farm
Cove, Sydney's Botanic Gardens
are an oasis of calm greenery in
the midst of the city's turmoil.
Governor Phillip's farm was
established here after the fleet's
arrival in 1788, and by July of
that year wheat, Australia's first
cereal crop, had been planted.
This was done at the expense of
local Aborigines, who were
displaced from important
ceremonial grounds on the
shores of Farm Cove. By 1816
part of the area had been

designated as gardens, which were greatly enlarged in 1831. Today's gardens contain many native Australian trees and plants such as eucalyptus, bottlebrush and rainforest trees, as well as exotic tropical imports from Africa, the Pacific, South East Asia and Central America. There is also a pyramid glasshouse containing tropical plants, and the National Herbarium. The grounds contain a pleasant restaurant and a good visitors centre and bookshop which has leaflets describing various garden walks. Guided tours of the Gardens are given on most days.

Within the Gardens area, but not open to the public, is NSW Government House, an 1845 Gothic revival mansion which is the official residence of the Governor of New South Wales.
Open: Daily, 08.00hrs to sunset. Visitors centre, Monday to Friday 10.00-16.00hrs; weekends 12.00-17.00hrs.
The Gardens are on the Sydney Explorer bus route

Central City Area

Many of the old city landmarks have been retained and add a much-needed dose of history to what is otherwise a very modern city. The central area contains the main shopping arcades and department stores.

◆◆◆
THE AUSTRALIAN MUSEUM
College Street
The country's largest collection of natural history and ethnographic displays is housed here in an 1849 building which has been greatly extended. Australia's unique wildlife is a

highlight, and there is an excellent, illuminating display on the Aborigines of Australia. Other galleries contain exhibits of Pacific Island culture, birdlife and the marine world. Special exhibitions are held regularly and the museum has a good gift and book shop; free tours can also be arranged.
Open: Monday 12.00-17.00hrs; Tuesday to Sunday 10.00-17.00hrs.
Train to Museum station; on the Sydney Explorer bus route

◆◆
DAVID JONES' DEPARTMENT STORE
corner of Castlereagh, Market and Elizabeth Streets
While in the central shopping area, it is worth looking into David Jones' store. The building dates from 1927, but recent renovations have turned it into a glossy marble, brass and glass creation which has earned it the title 'the most beautiful store in the world'. In addition to uniformed doormen, the store features huge floral displays and a grand piano which is played at intervals throughout the day.

◆◆
HYDE PARK
between Elizabeth and College Streets
Decreed as public land by Governor Phillip in 1792, this 41 acre area was proclaimed Hyde Park in 1810 and has been used for recreation ever since. Laid out in formal style, with geometric flower beds and pathways intersecting lawns, the park is popular with city office workers at lunchtimes and is often packed with photo-

A view from Sydney Tower of Hyde Park, which extends from Queen's Square to Liverpool Street and was first used for military drill, cricket and horseracing

snapping tourists. At the southern end, past the Park Street intersection, the Anzac War Memorial is a tribute to Australian soldiers. A photographic exhibition is open Monday to Saturday, from 10.00-16.00hrs and on Sunday from 13.00-16.00hrs.
Train to St James station

MARTIN PLACE

To the north of Sydney Tower towards Circular Quay, Martin Place stretches east to west,

from Macquarie Street to George Street, and is the city's largest plaza, with fountains, statues and a wide range of architectural styles. The Sydney General Post Office dates from 1874 and is an imposing sandstone building, in the Victorian Renaissance style, while at the other end of the scale, the MLC Centre is a 1978 office tower and shopping centre. Martin Place also has an amphitheatre which is the location for free concerts from 12 noon to 14.00hrs on weekdays, and the plaza is a good place to sit and watch the city's office workers making the most of their lunch break.
Train to Martin Place station

◆◆◆
QUEEN VICTORIA BUILDING

George Street (between Market and Druitt Streets)

The Queen Victoria Building, now an attractively restored, elegant four-storey shopping centre, has a long and interesting history. Taking up a whole city block, the massive Romanesque style Victorian building was completed in 1898 to celebrate Queen Victoria's golden jubilee and was originally built to house fruit and vegetable markets in the lower levels, with offices and shops above. After the relocation of the city markets, the building became, at various times, offices, the home of the city library and the Sydney County Council base. Thankfully the building has survived long periods of neglect and even threats to demolish it, and

The recently restored Queen Victoria Building, a shopping and architectural wonderland, is near Town Hall station

between 1984 and 1986 A$75 million was spent on restoration and refurbishment. The beautiful stained glass windows and tiled floors are exceptional features.
Open: daily
Train to Town Hall station

◆
ST ANDREW'S CATHEDRAL
George Street
Right next to the Town Hall, the city's Anglican cathedral was begun in 1837 and consecrated in 1868. It is a small perpendicular Gothic structure, made of Sydney sandstone and designed by Edmund Blacket, Sydney's most well-known church architect.
Open: daily

◆
ST MARY'S CATHEDRAL
College Street
Right across Hyde Park from David Jones, the city's Roman Catholic cathedral was constructed between 1868 and 1882 and is built of sandstone in the Gothic revival style. The interior is impressive, particularly for its heavily tinted stained glass windows.
Open: daily
Train to St James station

◆◆
STRAND ARCADE
between Pitt Street Mall and George Street
Until the restoration of the QVB (Queen Victoria Building), this was the pride of the city's shopping centre. A 1976 fire destroyed much of the arcade, but it has been faithfully restored to its original 1891 classical revival glory. It is worth visiting, not only for its three tiers of excellent shops, but to view the tiles, beautiful cast iron lacework, stained glass and period feel. The arcade is open 24 hours, with the shops following normal shopping hours.

◆◆◆
SYDNEY TOWER
Centrepoint, Market Street
The very best way to view Sydney's layout is from the top of one of its most modern, and certainly the tallest, buildings. Sydney Tower (1,000ft, 305m) is the city's most distinctive landmark, and one that can be seen from many miles distant. Completed in 1981, the tower is supported by a web of cables which are fixed to the Centrepoint building far below, and the view from the top is truly astounding. The 360° panorama includes all of the city and harbour, Botany Bay to the south, and even as far away as the Blue Mountains, over 50 miles (90km) to the west. It is by far the best way to get your bearings and understand the city's layout — the view at night is particularly spectacular. The tower also has two restaurants, one of which revolves, and a shop and information centre.
Open: Monday to Saturday 09.30-21.30hrs; Sunday and holidays 10.30-18.30hrs

◆
SYDNEY TOWN HALL
George Street
Just across the road from the QVB, Sydney's Town Hall is a solidly Victorian building, begun in 1868 and one of the rapidly disappearing landmarks of this era. The sandstone faced building is topped by a clock

tower and houses the Sydney City Council offices, as well as several halls. Free concerts are often given in the main hall.
Open: Monday to Friday 09.00-17.00hrs, and for concerts.
Train to Town Hall station

Darling Harbour

Once the harbour region's equivalent of a slum and a real city eyesore, the old Darling Harbour seaport has undergone a stunning transformation since 1984. The area has been completely revitalised and remodelled to form a shopping and convention centre with museums, exhibition halls and outdoor recreation areas such as Tumbalong Park and the attractive Chinese Garden. The

Elegant and stylish Darling Harbour

old Pyrmont Bridge, which dates from 1902, has been restored and now acts as a pedestrian walkway between the city and Darling Harbour. Above this, the new Monorail runs as part of its continuous loop around the southern city and Darling Harbour areas. Despite vigorous public protest the privately owned line went ahead, and although it doesn't look so bad in the open spaces here, it really becomes an eyesore once it hits the main city streets. Darling Harbour has a good shopping complex and some excellent bars, cafés and restaurants, many of which have outdoor eating areas. The complex also features weekend entertainment. All the following attractions can be reached by the Monorail from city stops: Elizabeth and Liverpool Streets, and Pitt Street near the Hilton Hotel.

◆◆
CHINATOWN
Dixon Street area, Haymarket
At the southern end of Darling Harbour, Chinatown forms an interesting and colourful contrast to most of Sydney's streets. Sydney's Chinese population moved to this part of the city from The Rocks area in the early years of this century, and it is now full of restaurants, Chinese food shops and shopping centres. Chinese New Year celebrations in January/ February are very colourful.
Monorail to the Haymarket station, or access via George Street buses

◆◆
CHINESE GARDEN
This attractive garden area was designed by landscape architects from China and features a pagoda, pavilions, paths, bridges and lakes in the traditional Chinese garden style. Appropriately, it is situated at the Chinatown end of the Darling Harbour.

◆◆
THE JAMES CRAIG and KANANGRA
These two ships are moored at Darling Harbour and are open to the public. The *James Craig* (1874), now only a hulk, was one of the three masted barques once commonly used in Sydney. The *Kanangra* is a restored and brightly painted 1912 Sydney ferry.

◆◆◆
NATIONAL MARITIME MUSEUM
This A$30 million project, nearing completion, will contain dozens of exhibits which recreate Australia's maritime history.

◆◆◆
POWERHOUSE MUSEUM
500 Harris Street, Ultimo
This recently renovated 1899 old power station and tram depot adjoins the southern end of Darling Harbour and contains the Museum of Applied Arts and Sciences' vast collection of material which dates back to the 1880s. The scale of this A$20 million enterprise is enormous — exhibits are housed in the cavernous old engine and boiler houses, as well as a new entrance hall and display building. The museum focuses on science, technology, decorative arts and social history, and includes many 'hands-on' displays which encourage viewer participation. Audiovisual presentations, sound effects and holograms complete the hi-tech picture. It is entertaining and educational and great fun for both kids and adults.
Open: Daily 10.00-17.00hrs.
Monorail to the Haymarket, or via Darling Harbour

◆◆◆
SYDNEY AQUARIUM
Pier 26, Darling Harbour
This new aquarium complex features special displays on the theme of Australian river and marine life (see also page 104).

HISTORIC SUBURBS

Although many of Sydney's historic sites are located around The Rocks and City areas, there is a great deal to see in the various suburbs of the city. Some, such as Balmain and Paddington, are interesting merely for their architecture and unique atmosphere.

Elizabeth Bay and Kings Cross

While in the Elizabeth Bay area, walk around streets such as Macleay and Victoria Streets, Potts Point, which are full of beautiful old Sydney terraced houses, complete with their distinctive iron lacework balconies and fences. Kings Cross, now a somewhat sleazy strip and sex club area, was once Sydney's most bohemian suburb and is still interesting for its old buildings and sidewalk cafés.

◆◆◆
ELIZABETH BAY HOUSE

Onslow Avenue, Elizabeth Bay
This gracious colonial mansion is located on the outskirts of Kings Cross and was built by architect John Verge for the Colonial Secretary, Alexander Macleay, from 1835 onwards. The house is Sydney's most elegant reminder of a bygone era and occupies a fine position overlooking the harbour; the grounds which once stretched right down to Elizabeth Bay are now covered with old style apartment buildings and large homes. The house has been restored and carefully furnished in mid-19th century style and has a wonderful central oval

saloon and winding staircase.
Open: Tuesday to Sunday 10.00-16.30hrs. Admission charge.
Train to Kings Cross; also on the Sydney Explorer bus route

Hunters Hill

The ferry trip to Hunters Hill, on the north side of the harbour and west of the bridge, is interesting in itself. You will pass suburbs such as Balmain, Birchgrove and Greenwich and see a very different aspect of the harbour. Once at Hunters Hill, walk around and see how the other half live!

◆◆
VIENNA COTTAGE

38 Alexandra Street, Hunters Hill
Built by shoemaker John Hellman in 1871, Vienna Cottage is a fine example of the small stone tradesmen's cottages which sprang up in the Hunters Hill area in the late 19th century. Apart from its architectural merit, the cottage includes displays on the history of Hunters Hill, now an expensive and desirable suburb.
Open: Saturday 14.00-16.00hrs; Sunday 11.00-16.00hrs.
Ferry from Circular Quay to Valentia Street wharf

La Perouse and Botany Bay

At the southern edge of modern Sydney, bleak, windswept Botany Bay is where colonial Australia began life. Captain James Cook and the *Endeavour* first sailed into the Bay in April 1770 and opened up the possibility of colonising this new found land with a convict population. This area has several monuments which commemorate the voyages of

Cook and other 18th-century explorers.

◆◆
CAPTAIN COOK'S LANDING PLACE HISTORIC SITE
Cape Solander Drive, Kurnell Peninsula
At the southern end of Botany Bay, the Kurnell Peninsula is now the province of oil refineries and heavy industry, but in 1770 was the point where Captain Cook and his party first set foot on Australian soil. Cook spent eight days here,

The many old, carefully restored houses in Elizabeth Bay make the area a particularly rewarding one to explore

confronting hostile Aborigines and collecting flora and fauna specimens, before continuing his journey. Monuments such as the Captain Cook Obelisk, erected in 1870, commemorate these events. A visitors centre, museum and walking trails are other attractions.
Open: weekends and public holidays 10.30-17.00hrs; weekdays 10.30-16.30hrs.
Train to Cronulla, then bus 67

◆◆
LA PEROUSE MONUMENTS
Anzac Parade, La Perouse
At the northern end of Botany Bay there is a Monument to Comte de la Perouse, a French

explorer who arrived in Botany Bay just six days after the First Fleet in 1788. The French left to continue their around the world journey, but were lost at sea and never seen again. The nearby Old Cable Station was built in 1882 to house telegraph line operators working on the line from Australia to New Zealand, and is now a La Perouse museum. The Macquarie Watchtower dates from the 1820s and was erected to keep a watch on frequent smuggling activities in Botany Bay. Off shore, Bare Island Fort is now linked to the mainland by an early 20th-century bridge, and is the site of an 1881 fort and 1889 military barracks. Once the

A Paddington house with its beautifully restored ironwork

British troops were sent home in 1870 the colony became responsible for its own security, and the Botany Bay defences were strengthened under the threat of attacks by the French and Russians. The fort has had little military importance, however, and its guns have never been fired in anger.
Bare Island Fort open: daily 9.00-15.00hrs.
All monuments can be reached by bus 393 from Railway Square, or 394 from Circular Quay

Paddington

Paddington's significance as an important preserve of Sydney's history is evident in the fact that the entire suburb has been defined as a conservation area by the National Trust.
Originally a sandy heathland, the first road through the area was built by Governor Macquarie in 1811, and it only became important once the Victoria Barracks were built in 1841. After this time, houses began to spring up, and by 1891 over 18,000 people lived here.

JUNIPER HALL
248 Oxford Street, Paddington
This simple two-storey colonial house was built from the profits of a gin distillery in 1824 and is the oldest domestic building still in existence east of Sydney's city. The family home of Robert Cooper was later used as a child welfare institution and now houses the Australian Museum of Childhood. This collection of 19th- and 20th-century children's toys, books and illustrations is housed upstairs, while the street level National Trust shop sells

some interesting Australiana.
Open: Tuesday to Saturday 10.00-16.00hrs
Bus 380 from Circular Quay, or 378 from Railway Square

◆◆
VICTORIA BARRACKS
Oxford Street, Paddington
These military barracks were the first buildings in what was once described by Governor Arthur Phillip as 'a kind of heath, poor, sandy and full of swamps'. It is hard to believe today! Built of Sydney sandstone, the two-storey Barracks complex was begun in 1841 and is an excellent example of colonial style 19th-century military architecture. The complex is still occupied by the Army and includes a military museum. Tours include the museum, barracks and pleasant grounds.
Open: Tuesdays only, 10.00hrs.
Bus 380 from Circular Quay, or 378 from Railway Square

Parramatta
The nation's second oldest settlement, 15 miles (24km) to the west of Sydney city, Parramatta was created just a few months after the Sydney Cove site in November 1788 and is full of history. Today the area is an important commercial and industrial centre, but in its early days it overshadowed Sydney Cove as the social and cultural hub of the fledgling colony; the first Government House was built here rather than in Sydney itself. The reason for the district's importance was that it had the fertile farming land which Sydney Cove lacked, and which was vital to support the near-starving population. Today

Parramatta has many important sites and buildings, including the country's oldest cemetery, St John's, and it is worth spending a full day here.

◆◆◆
ELIZABETH FARM
70 Alice Street, Parramatta
Once the home of agricultural pioneers John and Elizabeth Macarthur, Elizabeth Farm shows how an English-style cottage developed into a dwelling more suitable for Australian climatic conditions. Features such as the shady verandah were necessary to combat the fierce summer sun, and became a distinctive aspect of Australian architecture. Begun in 1793, the cottage contains remnants of the oldest European building in Australia and is now furnished in the style of that period.
Open: Tuesday to Sunday 10.00-16.30hrs
Train from Central or Town Hall to Parramatta

◆◆◆
EXPERIMENT FARM COTTAGE
9 Ruse Street, Parramatta
The land on which the building stands is as interesting as the cottage itself. Convict farmer James Ruse was the first man in the colony to prove that he could become self-sufficient and as a reward, Governor Phillip granted him the land in 1792. It was Australia's first land grant. Colonial Surgeon John Harris then purchased the land from Ruse in 1793 and built his cottage, which has been restored and is furnished in period style.
Open: Tuesday to Thursday,

Sunday 10.00-16.00hrs
Train from Central or Town Hall

◆◆◆
OLD GOVERNMENT HOUSE
Parramatta Park, Parramatta
Now under National Trust care, Old Government House is the nation's oldest public building, dating from 1799 but greatly extended by Governor Macquarie in 1816. In the early years of the colony this was the official Vice Regal residence; while convicts toiled at Sydney Cove, the glitterati of New South Wales were enjoying the beginnings of high society out here at Rose Hill, the early name for Parramatta. The house now contains an important and interesting collection of pre-1850 Australian furniture.
Open: Tuesday to Thursday, and Sunday 10.00-16.00hrs
Train from Central or Town Hall

Vaucluse
Vaucluse is one of the city's most pleasant suburbs, containing large and expensive homes, tree-lined streets, and harbour beaches like Nielsen Park and Parsley Bay, as well as a small slice of National Park.

◆◆
VAUCLUSE HOUSE
Olola Avenue
This 1830s Gothic-style house was the home of William Charles Wentworth, a noted explorer, barrister and statesman. Set in 27 acres of gardens and parkland, the 15-room house includes a lavishly decorated suite of entertaining rooms, most of which are furnished in mid-19th century style. Tea rooms serve

Vaucluse House is important for its historic memories – the Constitution of New South Wales was drawn up here – and for its furniture and paintings

Devonshire teas, and the gardens are a perfect picnic spot. The estate has its own harbourside beach.
Open: Tuesday to Sunday 10.00-16.30hrs. Admission charge.
Bus 325 from Circular Quay

Balmain
Balmain grew up as a working class suburb to house the many boat builders, wharf workers and tradesmen connected with the shipping industry – the area is just west of the bridge and on a peninsula which juts out into Port Jackson. It is full of narrow

streets which contain some of Sydney's most picturesque houses: terraces complete with iron lacework and small, free-standing weatherboard homes. There are also many pubs and the Saturday market. Many of the original working class locals have sold up and moved out of the area, leaving it free for the trendies to move in and renovate. The best way to reach Balmain is by a short ferry ride from Circular Quay.

Double Bay
At the opposite end of the scale, Double Bay is one of the city's most exclusive suburbs. This harbourside area reeks of money, with large houses and old-style apartment buildings, a

HISTORIC SUBURBS

yacht club, pleasant leafy streets and parks, and some of Sydney's most upmarket shops. Here you will find the outlets of top Australian designers, imported and expensive French and Italian shoes, and just about anything else that costs a lot of money. Double Bay also has many cafés where it is fun to sit and watch the world go by, albeit a well-heeled one. Just up the road, towards Rose Bay, Redleaf Pool is a popular harbour beach, and nearby Trumper Park has excellent tennis courts. You can get to Double Bay by bus 324 or 325 from Circular Quay, or by train to Edgecliff and then a short walk.

Watsons Bay

Watsons Bay's location just beneath South Head at the entrance to the harbour made it strategically important and one of Sydney's earlier settlements. The road from Sydney Cove was built in 1811 and there are still some cottages dating back to the 1840s. The one-time military base and fishing village is now visited for its views from South Head, two beaches, wonderful outlook over the harbour and the famous Watsons Bay Hotel which has a packed-to-capacity beer garden. During the week, Watsons Bay is reached by bus number 324 or 325 from Circular Quay, but at the weekend there is a ferry service from the Quay, which also calls in at Taronga Zoo and Rose Bay.

Other Suburban Attractions

◆◆
HALL OF CHAMPIONS

State Sports Centre, Underwood Road, Homebush
It is appropriate that a city so obsessed with sport should have a tribute to the achievements of its sporting greats. At the State Sports Centre, which has excellent indoor and outdoor facilities, the Hall of Champions covers sporting achievements from 1876 to the present day.
Open: daily, 08.30-17.00hrs
Train to North Strathfield

◆◆
SYDNEY MARITIME MUSEUM

Birkenhead Point, Drummoyne
Formed in 1965 with the intention of preserving historic ships in working order, this indoor/outdoor museum is part of the Birkenhead Point shopping, market and marina complex. Several craft moored at the wharf are open for inspection, while the indoor museum contains an exhibition of interesting maritime artefacts
Open: Monday 13.30-17.00hrs; Tuesday to Sunday 10.00-17.00hrs; admission charge.
Ferry from Circular Quay West

◆◆
SYDNEY TRAMWAY MUSEUM

Princes Highway, Loftus
Sydney's once widespread tram network died in the 1960s, but a volunteer society has restored some of the original vehicles and created this museum. It contains around 30 tramcars, some of which date back to the last century, and there is also the opportunity to ride a tram along a short stretch of track.
Open: Wednesday 09.30-15.30hrs; Sunday and public holidays 10.00-17.00hrs; admission charge.
Train to Loftus station

Windsurfing in the harbour will give you a splendid view of the city

THE GREAT OUTDOORS

Much of the city's appeal lies in its parks, beaches and waterways, its feeling of space, and the celebration of life in the great outdoors.

Waterways

◆◆◆
SYDNEY HARBOUR

There is little doubt in anyone's mind that Sydney Harbour or, more correctly, Port Jackson (named by Captain Cook in 1770) is the jewel of the city. It is what makes Sydney so special and so much less like a big city than it could appear. The harbour is really a series of connecting waterways: west of the bridge, the Parramatta River; to the northwest, the Lane Cove River; to the north, Middle Harbour and Port Jackson itself. Harbour scenery varies from red-roofed hillsides to the cityscapes of the CBD and North Sydney, quiet sandy coves and dramatic sandstone cliffs. Harbour traffic itself creates an interesting spectacle — huge container ships, cruise boats, ferries, yachts, water taxis and fishing boats all vie for space. Thankfully, large stretches of the foreshore of this drowned river valley are classified as national park, as are some of the harbour islands, and today we still have some remnants of native vegetation in these protected areas.

There are many tours and cruises which the visitor can take and the harbour has many foreshore walks and vantage points. From the southern shore, good views are obtained from

THE GREAT OUTDOORS

Mrs Macquarie's Point in the Domain, Nielsen Park at Vaucluse and from Watsons Bay. On the north side, Cremorne Point, Kirribilli, Taronga Park Zoo and Bradleys Head all give good views. The harbour islands are also worth visiting. Fort Denison, off Farm Cove, was originally used by Aborigines as a fishing spot, and later as a base for marooning particularly disobedient convicts. The current fort dates from 1855. The Maritime Services Board operates cruise/tours to Fort Denison (tel: 27 2733 Monday to Friday, 27 6606 at weekends). Goat Island, off Balmain, has a long maritime history and can also be visited (tel: 240 2036), while Rodd, Shark and Clarke Islands are all administered by the National Parks and Wildlife Service.

Beaches

Harbour beaches are popular swimming and picnicking spots. On the southside: at Vaucluse, Nielsen Park and Parsley Bay, and the Watsons Bay beaches such as Camp Cove and Lady Jane. North of the harbour at Mosman, Obelisk (a nude beach) and Balmoral are good spots. All beaches are served by public transport; tel: 954 4422 for details.

There is also a multitude of ocean beaches fringing the entire Sydney region from Palm Beach in the north to Cronulla in the south. These excellent sandy beaches have been experiencing pollution problems recently, but are still an integral part of a Sydney visitor's intinerary. In summer,

take note of the position of the flags and swim only between them. Ocean beaches are patrolled by lifeguards, so rescue is at hand if you get into trouble! Sharks are less of a problem than marine stingers.

North of the Harbour

◆◆
AVALON
A good surf beach which has a rock pool for kids and is easily accessible from the main road. *Buses 188 to 190 from Wynyard*

◆◆
COLLAROY
Ideal for families, with an ocean pool and a children's play area. *Bus 181-190 from Wynyard, or by ferry to Manly, then bus 155 or 157*

◆◆◆
MANLY
A real seaside town atmosphere with fish and chips, shops to browse in and a vast surf beach. The ferry or hydrofoil ride from Circular Quay is a pleasure in itself. Manly's other attractions include a fun pier and Underwater World.

◆◆
NEWPORT
Also good for surfing and has a nice shopping centre. *Bus 188-190 from Wynyard*

South of the Harbour

◆◆◆
BONDI
Sydney's most famous beach, and one that no tourist should miss. On summer weekends it is crowded with surfers, families, tourists and just sightseers who all soak up the sun, sea and

seaside town atmosphere. There are plenty of shops, pubs and good cafés and restaurants. *Train to Bondi Junction and then bus 380, or bus 380 from Circular Quay and Oxford Street*

◆◆
BRONTE

Very popular with families, as it has an ocean pool and a large park area behind the beach which is perfect for picnics and barbecues. *Train to Bondi Junction station, then bus 378*

◆◆
COOGEE

A large beach with pubs and shops in the suburb's centre and

The most famous of Sydney's beaches, mile-long Bondi is very commercial; it can also get very crowded

popular with both surfers and families. *Bus 372 from Railway Square, or 373/4 from Circular Quay*

◆
CRONULLA

The city's most southerly beach, and at over 6 miles (10km) long, also the longest. It is at the southern end of Botany Bay and a visit here can be combined with a trip to the area's historic sites (see pages 40-3). *Train to Cronulla station, then bus 66 or 67*

◆◆
TAMARAMA

south of Bondi

A small beach, popular with the young and trendy. The water can be treacherous here, so it is not good for families. From Tamarama you can take a lovely

clifftop walk to Bondi.
Train to Bondi Junction, then bus 391

Parks

Sydney is well endowed with green open spaces in which to walk, sit, jog or play sports. In addition to The Domain, Royal Botanic Gardens and Hyde Park (see pages 33-4) and the more distant National Parks (see following chapter), there are some other pleasant parks in the city area.

◆◆◆
CENTENNIAL PARK
off Oxford Street, Woollahra
Originally named Sydney Common and used as grazing grounds, the park became fully established in 1888, Sydney's centennial year. In January 1901 the ceremony which established Federation, the forming of the Australian Commonwealth, took place in the park. Among its grasslands, trees, ponds and sports fields locals take picnics, ride bikes or horses, jog or just relax. The park has a classy newish café — the Centennial Park Café — which serves breakfast, teas and lunch.
Bus 380 from Circular Quay

◆◆
LANE COVE RIVER STATE RECREATION AREA
off Delhi Road, Ryde
If you are on the northside, don't miss this area of beautiful natural bushland which contains the river, picnic and recreation areas and a wide variety of river birds. Boats and canoes are available for hire.
Buses 254, and 285-90 go to the Lane Cove area from Wynyard

◆◆
RUSHCUTTERS BAY PARK
off Bayswater Road, Rushcutters Bay
Rushes for Sydney Cove's early thatched dwellings were cut here from the earliest days of the colony, and the area was occupied by Aborigines for many decades after the arrival of the white man. The area is now a pleasant park, adjacent to Kings Cross, with tennis courts and good views of the forest of masts which make up the fleet of the Cruising Yacht Club — the starting point of the annual Sydney to Hobart yacht race.
Bus 324 or 325 from Circular Quay, or walk from Kings Cross

Weathered sandstone cliffs in the Blue Mountains

EXCURSIONS OUT OF TOWN

Sydney is surrounded by many regions of historical interest and natural beauty which are all within reach during a day trip. Some trips will need a couple of days or longer to fully appreciate the region. As the Sydney region is so large some places such as Palm Beach, even though within the outer Sydney boundary, are included in this section. For additional information on any of the following areas, contact the NSW Travel Centre (tel: 231 4444). Most of the places described in this section are accessible by public transport, but for touring the regions a car is essential (see page 112 for car hire details). Coach tours

also take in all the areas listed if you prefer not to drive.

◆◆◆
BLUE MOUNTAINS

west — 63 miles/100km
One of Sydney's most popular recreational areas, the Blue Mountains (hills would be a more apt description) area is mostly classified as national park and offers excellent opportunities for bushwalking, rockclimbing, horseriding or just sightseeing. (See also page 62.) The mountains are essentially a river-dissected sandstone plateau — an effect which has created some dramatic canyons and valleys, all of which are lined with gum trees. It is a vision of Australia's bushland as it was when first explored by the white man in the early 1800s. The Mountains area is full of small, picturesque towns such as Katoomba, Leura and Mount Victoria, complete with teashops, art galleries, antique shops and delightful, old-fashioned guesthouses. Nearby Jenolan Caves are also worth visiting. Winter is the perfect time to visit, when log fires and chilly nights (sometimes even snow) make a striking contrast to Sydney's still mild days. A weekend trip is recommended, especially as a visit to Richmond and Windsor (see below) can easily be combined with the Mountains.

◆◆
CANBERRA/ACT

southwest — 185 miles/300km
Unless you fly, it needs at least a weekend visit to cover both the 370 mile (595km) round trip to the national capital and the

sights once you get there. It is also a good idea to combine a visit to the Southern Highlands with the Canberra trip, if you have the time.

Until 1913 Canberra was just a patch of unimportant farming land in southern New South Wales. It became the site for a national capital as a result of the constant rivalry between Sydney and Melbourne for that honour. It is a planned city, occupied mostly by public servants and unlike anywhere else in Australia, with many attractions for a visitor. Parliament House, the Australian War Memorial (one of the nation's most-visited attractions), Lake Burley Griffin, the excellent National Gallery and several historic homesteads are all worth visiting, as are the Botanic Gardens. For more information, contact the Canberra Tourist Bureau, 64 Castlereagh Street (tel: 233 3666).

◆◆
CENTRAL COAST
north — 55 miles/88km
This area is another of Sydney's most popular 'escape' destinations with excellent surf beaches and the quiet, sheltered waterways of Brisbane Water. Two national parks — Bouddi and Brisbane Water — offer excellent bushwalking and fishing opportunities and some Aboriginal rock carvings, as well as the obvious boating activities. If you have time to head further north, The Entrance, Tuggerah Lake, Lake Macquarie (Australia's largest

seaboard lake), and miles of beautiful beaches right up to Newcastle are all worth visiting. Newcastle, NSW's second largest city and 105 miles (170km) from Sydney, is a good starting point for trips to the vineyards of the Hunter Valley (see below).

◆◆◆
HUNTER VALLEY
northwest — 100 miles/160km
Other than the quiet farmland scenery of this region, the Hunter's attraction is its vineyards and wineries, which produce excellent red and white wines. The many wineries around Cessnock and Pokolbin are all open for wine-tasting, tours and purchases — try Hungerford Hill, Rothbury Estate and Wyndham Estate. The more distant Upper Hunter area (145 miles/235km from Sydney) also has some good wineries, including the well respected Rosemount Estate. Other attractions include historic Wollombi village and some delightful country pubs and hotels.

◆◆
KU-RING-GAI CHASE NATIONAL PARK AND THE LOWER HAWKESBURY
north — 19 miles/30km
Although so close to the city, this is a beautiful unspoilt area of natural scrub forest and woodland which rings the lower reaches of the Hawkesbury River. Activities here include bushwalking, visiting Aboriginal carvings, and fishing. From Bobbin Head it is possible to go boating. A visitors' centre provides information on

Canberra, one of the world's most beautiful modern planned cities, attracts many visitors each year

ctivities within the national ark. (See also page 59.) You an either drive, or take a ferry o Bobbin Head from Palm each; the Palm Beach/Pittwater egion (see below) can be ombined with a visit to u-ring-gai.

◆◆◆
PALM BEACH AND PITTWATER
orth – 25 miles/40km
his is a great day trip, with all inds of possibilities. Palm each has a surf beach on one ide and, along Pittwater, some nore sheltered bathing spots

and good conditions for sailboarding or boating. There are some good walks, especially to the lighthouse on Barrenjoey Head, and it is interesting to just wander around and observe the lifestyle of the wealthy, and their substantial houses! From the Pittwater wharf various ferries ply the waterway and you can take a trip to Patonga Beach or Bobbin Head in Ku-ring-gai Chase National Park.
Round the day off with famous Palm Beach fish and chips on the beach. If you want to use public transport, the 190 bus from Wynyard takes you right to Palm Beach, the end of the line.

EXCURSIONS OUT OF TOWN

◆◆
RICHMOND, WINDSOR AND THE UPPER HAWKESBURY

northwest — 45 miles/72km
This pleasant rural region is also one of Sydney's oldest satellite settlements, which dates back to 1810 and was established to provide farming ground for the colony. Towns like Richmond and Windsor have retained many of their old buildings, like the sandstone St Matthews Church at Windsor, designed by Francis Greenway. The settlement of Ebenezer has Australia's oldest surviving place of worship in its 1809 church. From Windsor you can continue on to lovely, quiet areas such as the Cattai Recreation Area and Hawkesbury River villages like Wisemans Ferry. This region can easily be combined with a trip to either Parramatta or the Blue Mountains.

◆◆
ROYAL AND HEATHCOTE NATIONAL PARKS

south — 22 miles/36km
These two national parks — separated only by the southbound Princes Highway — take up a large part of Sydney's far southern region. Heathcote features woodland vegetation and is a good bushwalking area, while the Royal NP includes a long stretch of rugged coastline, large surf beaches, good fishing and bushwalks. (See also page 61.) Both parks can be reached by public transport: for Heathcote take the train to Waterfall or Heathcote stations, and for the Royal NP, the station of the same name.

◆◆
SOUTH COAST

south — 75 miles/120km
The south coast area includes more spectacular coastal scenery, as well as NSW's third largest city, Wollongong, which, although a port and industrial centre has some great beaches and the large Lake Illawarra just to the south. Further on, Kiama is a picturesque fishing and tourist town, first visited by explorer George Bass in 1797. If you have time, the scenery south of Kiama gets better and better, and at Jervis Bay (112 miles/180km from Sydney) you'll find a beautiful white sand and sparkling blue ocean 'away-from-it-all' haven. This is one of the best spots within 125 miles (200km) of Sydney.

◆◆◆
SOUTHERN HIGHLANDS

south — 86 miles/137km
This attractive rural region is more reminiscent of England than Australia, and makes a delightful destination for a day or, preferably, a weekend trip. Here you will find historic houses, old villages, small farms and some really excellent guesthouses, including a health farm. The 1820s dairying industry which developed here is still predominant, and there are old towns like Berrima with its 1830s buildings, teashops and antiques. You should also visit Kangaroo Valley and the rugged Morton National Park. A visit to this region can be combined with trips to the Royal National Park and the south coast.

PEACE AND QUIET

Wildlife and Countryside in and around Sydney

Southeast Australia contains some of the finest scenery in the whole continent, together with many of its more extraordinary animals. During a few weeks stay in Sydney, the visitor can easily see more than a hundred species of birds, marsupial mammals such as wallabies and

The eastern slopes of the Great Dividing Range are cloaked in rainforest; a tranquil haven from the bustle of Sydney

possums, and, from July to October, a wonderful display of colourful flowers on the coastal heaths.

Away from the coast, hills rise up towards the Great Dividing Range, an extensive chain of hills that runs almost the entire length of eastern Australia. Its eastern slopes are cloaked in forests full of exotic animals and tree ferns, while the western side lies in a rainshadow and merges into the vast open plains of the outback. To protect the finest areas from future development, New South Wales has a network of national

PEACE AND QUIET

parks, many of which are within an easy day's journey from the state capital. These are a haven both for the wildlife and for those with an interest in it, affording the visitor access to, and information about, the most unspoilt parts of New South Wales.

In and Around Sydney

Although some of the finest territory lies on the Great Dividing Range, which is a full day's drive inland, the wildlife and landscapes in and around the city itself are fascinating, the natural beauty often being complemented by the modern architecture of the city.

The Royal Botanic Gardens near the Opera House, the Taronga Zoo and formal parks within the city's boundary provide a range of semi-natural habitats which attract many species of bird. Black-faced cuckoo-shrikes forage among the foliage of colourful flowering trees and, almost invariably, kookaburras can be found perching in the low branches of trees, ever alert for the movement of insects and lizards.

Superb blue wrens are common, their blue crown, cheeks and shoulder feathers producing a dazzling effect when they catch the light. They forage on lawns and sometimes feed in the company of magpielarks, which are noisy black and white birds whose dueting calls between pairs of birds are a familiar sound of the bush. Small parties of lorikeets or sulphur-crested cockatoos are equally raucous and are occasionally seen in flight or

feeding among bushes in parks and gardens.

Strolling along Sydney's extensive waterfront anywhere from the harbour to Botany Bay, the visitor is sure to come across silver gulls. Sometimes these opportunistic birds become so daring that they mob passers-by at the slightest sign of food. Off shore, crested terns plunge-dive into the waters after fish while Australian pelicans feed in groups and sometimes roost communally on harbour walls and breakwaters.

The city even has its own national park — Sydney Harbour National Park — with spectacular cliffs and beautiful beaches which are within easy reach of the centre. Exposed sandstone headlands, buffeted by the Pacific Ocean, sometimes yield good views of passing seabirds such as giant petrels and albatrosses, and the soil here supports a wonderful array of heathland trees, shrubs and herbs. Crimson bottlebrushes, banksias and heathers vie with each other for beauty and attract a wide variety of insects and birds.

Birds of the Coast

The coast of New South Wales has much to offer the visitor with an interest in wildlife. Shells and other strandline debris make fascinating study, but it is perhaps the birds that are most interesting.

Harbours and waterfronts always have small parties of silver gulls in attendance. On uninhabited beaches these scavenging birds feed on animal remains washed up on

A sulphur-crested cockatoo dining off fruit and nuts is a fairly common sight in Sydney's parks

the beach, but their adaptable nature has enabled them to make use of man and they take scraps of fish or anything else that is even vaguely edible. Their silvery-grey wings, piercing white eyes and harsh, grating call make them easy to identify, but they are sometimes joined by larger Pacific and kelp gulls. The latter species is also a noisy bird and has a most distinctive 'yo-yo-yo' call. Another familiar bird of the coast is the Australian pelican, often seen swimming in harbours or roosting in large numbers on rocky outcrops and breakwaters. On land its gait is cumbersome and waddling but in the air it is masterful. Long lines of pelicans can be seen

PEACE AND QUIET

flying past headlands, often soaring to great heights or gliding on outstretched wings. It can be rewarding, during periods of strong, onshore winds, to watch the passage of seabirds past headlands. Several species of albatross are regularly seen, black-browed and wandering albatrosses being the most regular. Giant petrels, skuas, shearwaters, Australian gannets, terns and cormorants are also frequently seen, their numbers reflecting the wealth of marine life in the Pacific.

Along suitable beaches, migrant waders collect to feed and roost. Most are migrants from the northern hemisphere, breeding in Russia, China and North America, and while some continue their journeys further south, many stay from September to March. Curlew sandpipers and red-necked stints can be common and are sometimes joined by bar-tailed godwits, great knot or resident pied oystercatchers.

Southern giant petrel − one of the superb seabirds that you might see on the coast

Marshes and Wetlands

s with wetlands everywhere,
kes and marshes in New South
ales act like magnets to birds
ho are attracted to the
esh water to feed, drink and
the. There are marshes and
ools up and down the coast
d even some — such as those
ound Botany Bay — close to
dney itself. These coastal
eas lure waders, terns and
lls, being especially
portant at high tide when
rds of the seashore are
shed off their feeding
ounds. However, even the
ier regions of the state are not
thout water and these
come a refuge for both
ater-loving and dry country
ecies.

ing beyond the Great
viding Range and about 30
les (48km) north of West
yalong, Lake Cowal is a
eshwater haven on the edge of
e outback. As with other
rmanent water bodies in the
y country, it is not only a
p-off point for migrant
aders and passerines but also
me to year-round residents,
d 25 species of duck alone
e regularly seen on its waters.
erons, egrets and ibises stalk
e shallows in search of frogs
d fish, and whistling kites and
arsh harriers circle overhead.
arginal vegetation is home to
amorous reed warblers who
eave little nests out of the
ach of ground predators. The
armingly named willy wagtail
en feeds around the marshy
argins, using fenceposts as a
okout perch.

the open water, black ducks
d the occasional white-eyed

duck are often seen, but by far
the most unusual bird found on
inland lakes is the musk duck.
The males of these goose-sized
birds have a peculiar leathery
flap under the bill which is
expanded during display. This
ritual also involves a good deal
of splashing and noise and the
bizarre grunts and whistles are
frequently uttered all night long.
Marshes and pools along the
coast lure waders such as
curlew and sharp-tailed
sandpipers, plovers, godwits
and whimbrels. Since many of
them feed on the shoreline,
their numbers on the freshwater
pools fluctuate according to the
state of the tide. On the other
hand, masked plovers, with
their peculiar yellow wattles,
prefer the freshwater. On larger
areas of water, black swans,
freckled ducks and chestnut
teal dabble in the shallows.

**Ku-ring-gai Chase National
Park**

Twenty miles (32km) north of
Sydney lies the Ku-ring-gai
Chase National Park, an easy
drive from the city. Its
boundaries protect 35,000 acres
of outstanding sandstone
bushland and over 70 miles
(112km) of magnificent coastal
scenery, which is perhaps best
viewed from Commodore
Heights. From here,
commanding views up and
down the coast can be had with
a vista of wooded hills rising
away from the sea.
Like many of Australia's national
parks, Ku-ring-gai is geared up
for visitors, be they experienced
naturalists, enthusiastic hikers or
day-trippers simply out to

PEACE AND QUIET

admire the scenery. The information and interpretation centre at Bobbin Head is staffed by enthusiastic and knowledgeable rangers who can help with questions, while independent visitors can take advantage of the extensive network of tracks and trails which wind their way through the forest and bush.

The coastal heathlands of Ku-ring-gai can be just as colourful as those in the Royal National Park on the other side of Sydney. Banksias and

One of the many species of banksia, this one, coast Banksia, grows near the coast and attracts many birds and insects

bottlebrushes attract several species of honeyeater to feed on the nectar, as well as colourful butterflies and other insects. Small snakes and lizards, which scuttle through the undergrowth, sometimes fall victim to the ever-alert kookaburra, a frequently seen and heard resident of the park. While strolling through the forests, the visitor is serenaded by strange noises from the resident birds, frogs and insects. Perhaps most evocative is the explosive 'whipcrack' call of the aptly named eastern whipbird. It hops and jumps along the forest floor as it searches for insects, and with its long tail, it somewhat resembles a bulbul or a babbler.

By quietly strolling along one of the more remote tracks, visitors may come across yellow robins, yellow-throated scrub-wrens, whistlers or even one of the park's shy marsupial mammals, such as the swamp wallaby. King parrots and rainbow and scaly-breasted lorikeets are common and small parties are often seen hurtling through the woodland clearings in search of blossom trees which provide them with pollen, nectar and insects. At dusk, dollar birds become active, their circular white wing patches, from which their name derives, making them superficially similar to a nightjar in flight.

Royal National Park

Lying 20 miles (32km) to the south of Sydney, the Royal National Park contains over 70,000 acres of superb coastal scenery, forested hills and bushland. A network of roads allows exploration of the forests and beaches, and from boats hired in Audley, the adventurous visitor can admire the rainforests which cover the hillsides.

Founded in the 1880s as a reserve, the park acquired Royal status after the visit of Queen Elizabeth II in 1954. Its scenery and wildlife do much to

The Royal National Park is a wonderful place to spend a day trip from Sydney, particularly in spring and early summer when the wild flowers are in bloom

justify this honour and the park's species list contains hundreds of species of plant, bird and mammal. Although a popular day-trip from Sydney, the park is large enough to accommodate all-comers, especially since very few people stray far from the roads and parking areas. Where cliffs are exposed to the full force of the Pacific Ocean, the sandstone which underlies most of the Royal National Park supports a floral community known as coastal heath. Although the superficial appearance is rather similar to European heathland, the plants which comprise it are completely different.

PEACE AND QUIET

Spring in Australia, which from the point of view of flowering plants can last from July to October, produces a wonderful array of colour. The red flowers of the waratah, the New South Wales state emblem, vie with the evocatively named crimson bottlebrush and Christmas bells, and many species of heath. Perhaps most impressive of all, however, is the heath banksia with its large red and orange spikes. Fortunately, some plants bloom in the autumn and winter so there is something of interest throughout the year.

The sheltered coastal cliffs are cloaked in lush rainforests full of the sounds of tree frogs and exotic birds, set against a green backdrop of vines, creepers and palms. From Audley, roads and paths venture deeper into the forest where the forest floor and even the branches of the giant trees are covered with ferns and mosses. On the ground, male satin bowerbirds collect colourful objects to adorn their nesting bowers, while superb lyrebirds and Lewin's honeyeaters forage for food. The latter may even visit picnic tables, and in these open areas, the lucky visitor may also see wonga pigeons, lorikeets, kookaburras and superb blue wrens.

The Blue Mountains National Park

As part of the Great Dividing Range, the Blue Mountains were once an insurmountable barrier separating coastal Australia from the outback. At one time, the whole area would have been a high, sandstone plateau more than 3,000ft (1,000m) above sea level, but erosion by rivers and streams over countless millennia have carved deep gulleys and valleys into its surface.

Now all that remains of the original plateau are precipitous ridges and outcrops, such as those at Katoomba and Leura, but the isolation of these sandstone pinnacles and cliffs makes the scenery all the more dramatic. The spectacular view from these lookouts show ridges of hills stretching into the distance as far as the eye can see. Various shades of orange and red colour the sandstone and the glow in dawn or dusk sunlight is a memorable sight. Most of the national park's 243,000 acres lie in the valley of the Grose River, which is surrounded on all sides by imposing sandstone cliffs. All the best viewpoints can be reached by car, the cliff drive from Katoomba to Sublime Point itself being astonishing, but the vast majority of the park's area is accessible only on foot. Although this means that some considerable effort is required to explore the forested gulleys and valleys, the rewards are well worth it. In fact, the seclusion adds to the appeal of the park and also benefits the wildlife in no small way.

Dense forests cloak the valley bottoms and the less precipitous cliff faces, and many species of eucalyptus are found, including immense specimens of blue gum. The understorey is luxuriant and stream margins are thick with maiden-hair ferns and tree ferns. Duck-billed

Although shy and secretive, red-necked wallabies can often be spotted by sharp-eyed naturalists in the national parks around Sydney

platypuses can be seen at dawn and dusk using their curious beak-like mouths to sift animals from the silt and gravel of the stream beds, while in clearings, black-striped and red-necked wallabies and grey kangaroos cautiously feed. In the tree canopy above, nocturnal possums and sugar gliders are sometimes seen by observant visitors in the twilight, and yellow robins and crimson rosellas forage among the foliage. The beautifully marked Wonga pigeon feeds on the forest floor early in the morning or late in the afternoon and

some individuals can become remarkably tame. During the middle of the day, they generally sit among the branches uttering their incessant 'wonk' call.

Brisbane Water National Park

Forty miles (64km) north of Sydney, on the far side of Broken Bay, lies Brisbane Water National Park. The park boundary encloses nearly 19,000 acres of superb coastal and riverine scenery and fine examples of Aboriginal rock engravings. Eucalyptus woodlands abound, and pockets of rainforest with an understorey of tree ferns and figs cloak the ravines and gulleys, while the exposed remains of sandstone plateaux support colourful

coastal heathlands.
Among the eucalyptus
woodlands, birds such as
multi-coloured rainbow
lorikeets, musk lorikeets and
crimson and eastern rosellas
noisily feed among the foliage
and nest in cracks and holes in
ancient trees. Small parties
screech through the trees, often
flying so fast that it is difficult to
get more than a brief glimpse of
them.
In areas of open woodland, the
familiar kookaburra perches
among the branches; its loud,
laughing call is one of Australia's
best-known sounds. Despite the
fact that it shows no particular
preference for water, the
kookaburra is a member of the
kingfisher family, but instead of
fish, it catches lizards, snakes
and insects. From its perch it

*Kookaburra — the unmistakable
laughing call of this bird has
endeared it to generations of
Australians*

glides down at the first sign of
movement on the ground below.
From August to November, the
coastal heathlands of Brisbane
Water National Park are
covered in flowering bushes
and trees. Bottlebrushes and the
delightful lemon yellow flowers
of the coastal banksia attract
many insects and birds.
One family of Australian birds,
the honeyeaters, has evolved a
specially close relationship with
the flowers. They are
widespread throughout New
South Wales and several
species are commonly
encountered on the heathland.
It is fascinating to watch their
long tongues flicking in and out
of the flowers as they feed, and
because they are such active
blossom-feeders, they are
generally considered to be as
important as insects in the
pollination of flowers.

Warrumbungle National Park
The dramatic scenery of the
Warrumbungle National Park is
amongst the finest in eastern
Australia. The landscape is
dominated by volcanic features
with deep gorges and the
remains of craters. Most
impressive of all, however, are
the jagged lava plugs which
mark the cores of extinct
volcanoes. These erupted some
13 million years ago, the cones
themselves having long-since
been eroded away by the
elements. Although the park is
nearly 300 miles (480km) away
from Sydney, in the Orana
region of the state, those who
make the journey are rewarded
with views and wildlife
unrivalled in New South Wales.

*right bird in a bright tree. A
rainbow lorikeet in an Erythrina.
Lorikeets are usually found in
Eucalyptus woodlands*

The hills and mountains of the
Great Dividing Range, which
runs parallel with the eastern
coast of Australia, effectively
isolate the plants and animals on
either side. To the east, the hills
which run down to the coastal
plain receive plenty of rainfall
and the vegetation is lush. The
animals, too, are suited to this
climate and would have
difficulty surviving to the west,
where dry plains stretch into the
outback.

The 38,000 acres which
comprise Warrumbungle
National Park lie on this divide
and it is one of the few parks to
contain elements from both
geographical divisions. With the
land outside the park
boundaries coming under
increasing pressure from
agriculture, Warrumbungle is
rapidly becoming an isolated
refuge for the wildlife of the
surrounding countryside.
Trails and paths of varying
lengths criss-cross the park and
are designed to suit both the
casual rambler and the more
experienced hiker. Some, such
as the Pincham Trail, can be
completed in a day's easy
walking, while back-packers
can trek for several days to the
summits of Mount Exmouth or
Bluff Mountain.
Eucalyptus trees such as the
snow gum cloak many of the
hills, and in shady valleys
maiden-hair ferns and figs grow

PEACE AND QUIET

in lush profusion. Lorikeets, King parrots, cockatoos, and crimson rosellas are common and conspicuous among the trees, while red-necked wallabies and kangaroos move secretively among the ground vegetation. As evidence of the park's extraordinary mixture of species, small groups of emus are often seen patrolling the dry, open areas and sometimes come close to the camping sites. Other dry country species include spotted quail-dove, white-winged triller and red-backed kingfisher, the latter frequently being found miles from the nearest water.

Australia's Birds

For a continent the size of Australia, a list of breeding bird species of around 650 is comparatively small. This is a reflection of the small variety of different habitats and the uniform nature of much of the interior. However, this is easily compensated for by the extraordinary appearance and behaviour of birds like parrots, cockatoos, bowerbirds and honeyeaters.

As Sydney lies on the southeast coast of the continent close to the forests of the Great Dividing Range, visitors to the city can visit several different habitats and consequently experience some of the best birdwatching in Australia. To add to the interest, from September to March, the east coast of Australia also receives an influx of migrants from the northern hemisphere. Huge numbers of waders and terns throng suitable marshes and beaches,

making a fascinating spectacle Australia's largest bird is the emu, a flightless species which despite a concerted effort from 1930 to 1960 to exterminate it, is still widespread and common in open habitats such as Warrumbungle National Park. Like its African counterpart, the ostrich, it has sacrificed flight for running ability and has developed huge and powerful legs which will carry it at speeds of up to 30mph.

The forests of New South Wales are home to a variety of colourful parrots, cockatoos and lorikeets. Everything about them is conspicuous: most species are brightly coloured and they are all extremely noisy. Cockatoos and parrots have strong, hooked beaks and feed on seeds, fruits and nuts, while lorikeets have specially adapted brush-tipped tongues which they use to feed on the nectar and pollen in blossoms.

The rainforests around Sydney are home to one of Australia's most fascinating birds. In appearance, the brush turkey is just like a large, black hen but its breeding behaviour is bizarre. Instead of building a nest, the male constructs a huge mound of earth and leaves up to 13ft (4m) in diameter. The female then lays a dozen eggs which are buried in the mound and left to incubate for seven weeks, after which time the young dig their way to the surface and to freedom. During incubation, the male regulates the temperature of the mound by scraping and turning the soil thus ensuring that the eggs do not overheat.

Another of Australia's unmistakable national symbols, the koala is now, alas, an endangered species

Australian Mammals

Australia is a land full of strange and wonderful creatures, and none more so than its mammals. Their ancestors first colonised the continent around 70 million years ago. When the land bridge with the other continents was severed, the colonising mammals were left to evolve in isolation, and with such a wealth of habitat and range of environments, they proliferated into the vast array of species we see today. Dog-like carnivores evolved to prey upon small, rodent-like possums, and kangaroos and wallabies grazed the grass, occupying the same

PEACE AND QUIET

niche as deer and sheep elsewhere in the world. Despite millions of years of evolution, Australia's native mammals still have one thing in common: they are marsupials, or pouched mammals. Instead of giving birth to fully formed young, their offspring are born at an early stage of development which is completed in the mother's pouch. The young kangaroo, for example, is born after only 30 days when it weighs less than a gram. It does not leave the pouch until 250 days later, by which time it has become a real burden to its mother.

The echidna or spiny anteater is a fascinating animal which roots in the soil for insects. As its name suggests, it is covered in fearsome spines and when threatened, burrows into the ground with only the spines showing. The echidna's life cycle is even more extraordinary than its appearance, however, because it does not give birth to young but instead lays an egg. In common with its marsupial relatives, it transfers this to its pouch and after a week or so the young echidna hatches. This leaves the pouch ten weeks later when its spines are too painful for the mother to bear.

Australia's favourite mammal must surely be the koala. Now much reduced in numbers, this endearing animal is always associated with eucalyptus trees. It is a rather fussy eater, however, and will only take shoots of a certain age and then from only 20 of the 400 species

that occur in Australia. Not all Australia's mammals are as appealing, however. The wombat is a rather stubby animal which spends much of its time burrowing underground. Because of its subterranean habits, the pouch opens toward the tail-end so that it does not fill with soil.

Bowerbirds

Bowerbirds are related to birds of paradise and are found only in Australia and New Guinea. Although more sombre in appearance than their flamboyant relatives, bowerbirds have even more extraordinary courtship display and rituals which make use of the bird's architectural skills rather than colourful plumage. Satin bowerbirds are common in the forests of the Divide in southeast Australia, where their loud 'wee-oo' call is a familiar sound. They get their name from the elaborate avenue-like bower constructed by the male from twigs and grasses, the inside of which is plastered with charcoal and wood pulp.

The arena itself is adorned with colourful blue or yellow objects picked up from the forest floor, carefully arranged for the best effect. Formerly, these would have comprised flowers, insect wings and berries, but nowadays broken glass, plastic and pegs are favoured substitutes. When displaying to the female, the male holds one of the colourful objects in his beak and dances or sways as if in a trance; if she is sufficiently impressed, the female consents to mate.

Sautéed eel in sweet and sour sauce: 'Oz Nouveau' cuisine uses unusual flavourings and mixes of ingredients

FOOD AND DRINK

Eating Out

Australia has never been famous for its indigenous cuisine but, thankfully, Sydney's restaurants today offer an incredible variety of produce, and ways of cooking it. The country's policy of multicultural migration has led, especially over the last ten years, to a vast improvement in the type of restaurants and menus available in Sydney, and Asian food in particular is of an excellent standard. The city now has Japanese, Thai, Indonesian, Chinese, Malaysian, Kampuchean and Vietnamese restaurants in their hundreds, as well as European cuisines such as particularly good Italian, French, German, Spanish, Greek, Eastern European, and even Irish! There has been a revolution in Australian fare too.

Bistros and brasseries which serve 'Oz Nouveau' — a light and imaginative cuisine using Australia's fine range of seafoods, meats and other produce — are deservedly popular, while there is a huge number of seafood restaurants throughout the city. Restaurants in Sydney fall into two categories: licensed and BYO, which means Bring Your Own liquor. BYO status means that you avoid the large mark up on beer and wine and so eat out for considerably less. Most BYO restaurants are in the cheaper price range and they will charge a corkage fee of around 50 cents or a dollar per person. Eating out in Sydney is generally not expensive; the annual guide *Cheap Eats in Sydney* features over 750 restaurants where it is possible to eat two or even three courses for under A$22, which is certainly within most people's means. Some establishments add a surcharge on weekends, generally A$1 per person. Many restaurants close on Mondays and some on Sundays. Booking is recommended, especially on Friday and Saturday nights. Credit cards such as American Express, Visa, Mastercard and Diners are widely accepted, but not in some of the smaller, cheaper restaurants. Service charge is rarely included in the bill, and although tipping is not compulsory it is polite to leave 10 per cent of the bill if you feel satisfied with the service you have received.

The best central areas for a good choice of restaurant are: Chinatown in the city for Chinese food and *yum cha,* the Chinese weekend brunch; Darlinghurst, especially around Oxford and Victoria Streets, for cheap Asian and Italian fare; Kings Cross has a good range of steakhouses, brasseries and Asian restaurants; and the inner west suburb of Glebe for a selection of Asian and European. The CBD has some of the more expensive eateries, especially those in the top hotels like the Regent and Inter-Continental, as well as a large number of snack bars and cafés, which are mostly day-time only, to cater for city office workers.

Australian

If you are interested in dining in traditional Aussie style, try a counter lunch at one of the city's many pubs, which will consist of steak and chips or something similar, or visit **Phillip's Foote,** 101 George Street, The Rocks (tel: 241 1485), which offers a barbecue-your-own meat meal, accompanied by a selection of salads. It is a lot of fun and has an outdoor eating area. Licensed and open daily for lunch and dinner.

You do your own cooking here

Brasseries and Bistros

French style brasseries and bistros, which serve both food and drinks, often at outdoor tables, have gained a great deal of popularity in Sydney in the past few years. The food is generally French or Italian style, with some Oz Nouveau content and most of these restaurants fall into the medium price range. Note that many do not accept bookings — ring to check.

The **Bayswater Brasserie,** 32 Bayswater Road, Kings Cross (tel: 357 2749) is Sydney's most well-established and popular brasserie. It has an outdoor eating area and is open from lunch till late daily, with breakfast served at weekends; licensed. Two others in the Kings Cross area are the **Fountain Bistro,** 64 Macleay Street (tel: 356 3543), which has outdoor tables, is open for lunch and dinner daily, and also serves excellent breakfasts, licensed; and the **Macleay Street Bistro** at 73a Macleay Street, Potts Point. BYO and open from Tuesday to Saturday for lunch and dinner.

Ethnic Food

Any taste can be catered for, and, with the exception of Japanese restaurants, prices are extremely reasonable. Indian food is perhaps the least interesting of Sydney's Asian cuisines — you're better off aiming for the particularly good Thai food, or Vietnamese, Malaysian and Indonesian.

Chinese: Sydney has several expensive and very upmarket restaurants in this category. One of the best is **Choy's Jin Jiang,** Level 2, Queen Victoria Building, City (tel: 261 3388), where fine Szechuan and Shanghai food is served in elegant surroundings. It is open for lunch and dinner seven days. Licensed. There are two other Choy's establishments which are somewhat cheaper — **Choy's Inn** and **Choy's 1000 AD,** both located in Hay Street, Chinatown (tel: 211 4213 or 211 3050). The **Imperial Peking Harbourside** at 5 Circular Quay West, The Rocks (tel: 223 1128) is another upmarket Chinese restaurant which has a great location opposite the Opera House and specialises in seafood. It is licensed and open for lunch and dinner, seven days.

There is a host of cheaper eateries in Chinatown, including **Nine Dragons,** 39 Dixon Street (tel: 211 3661), **Tea House of the New August Moon,** 68-70 Dixon Street (tel: 212 4702) and **Golden Century,** 405 Sussex Street (tel: 212 3901). All are open for lunch and dinner daily and are licensed. The **Chinatown Centre** in Dixon Street, which is an arrangement of stalls serving a wide variety of Chinese and other Asian food, is cheap and cheerful; open daily from 09.00-21.00hrs.

Indian: Curry Bazaar at 132 Norton Street, Leichhardt (tel: 560 7957) and 334 Pacific Highway, Crows Nest (tel: 436 3620) are very reasonable, BYO and open Monday to Saturday. Another above average Indian is **Manjit's** at 2/67 Macleay Street, Potts Point (tel: 358 4595), which is BYO and open for

FOOD AND DRINK

lunch Monday to Friday; dinner seven days a week.

Indonesian: Two good ones in Darlinghurst are: the **Bali Inn,** 80 Oxford Street (tel: 331 3544), BYO and open for lunch Monday to Friday, dinner every day; and the **Borobudur,** 263 Oxford Street (tel: 331 3463) which is slightly more expensive. It's BYO and open for lunch Tuesday to Friday, dinner Monday to Saturday.

Japanese: Sydney's best and most expensive is the **Suntory,** 529 Kent Street, City (tel: 267 2900), serving exquisite food in equally nice surroundings. Open for lunch and dinner, Monday to Saturday, and licensed. Two that are much cheaper are: the **Fuji Tempura Bar,** 18 Ash Street, City (tel: 231 1740), which specialises in Tempura and is open from Monday to Friday for lunch, Wednesday to Friday for dinner, BYO; and **Origami,** 150 Liverpool Street, East Sydney (tel: 331 3733), which has fine food at reasonable prices. Open for dinner Tuesday to Saturday and also BYO.

Kampuchean: The city's three **Mekong** restaurants serve a combination of Kampuchean and Chinese food at unbelievably cheap prices. Big helpings and fast service are a bonus at these establishments which are all open every day from 11.00-21.30hrs, BYO. They are located at 711 George Street, City (tel: 211 0221), 570 Oxford Street, Bondi Junction (tel: 387 1668) and 394 Anzac Parade, Kingsford (tel: 662 4006).

Malaysian: The **Malaya,** a cheap and popular Sydney institution,

can be found in two locations: 761 George Street, City (tel: 211 0946) and 86 Walker Street, North Sydney (tel: 92 4306). Both are licensed and open for lunch and dinner, every day.

Thai: Definitely Sydney's most up and coming cuisine, which is delicate, but spicy enough to suit the most avid chilli lover. There are dozens to choose from, but some of the best are: the **Thai Orchid,** 628 Crown Street, Surry Hills (tel: 698 2097), licensed and open for lunch Monday to Friday, dinner every night; **Narai Thai,** 346 Victoria Street, Darlinghurst (tel: 331 1390), open for lunch Tuesday to Friday and dinner nightly, licensed; the **Tara Thai,** 39a Elizabeth Bay Road, Elizabeth Bay (tel: 357 1036), licensed and open Tuesday to Sunday for lunch and dinner; and the **Thai Silver Spoon** at 203 Oxford Street, Darlinghurst (tel: 360 4669). This is BYO and open for lunch Tuesday to Friday, dinner seven days a week.

Vietnamese: Again, lots of good, cheap restaurants which serve this kind of food. Try **Chu Bay,** 312a Bourke Street, Darlinghurst (tel: 331 3386), BYO and open for dinner Tuesday to Sunday; and **Kim-Van** at 147 Glebe Point Road, Glebe (tel: 660 5252), which is arguably Sydney's best Vietnamese. It is open for dinner every day and is BYO.

European

Other than French and Italian restaurants, which deserve their own more detailed listings, there are many interesting European style restaurants in Sydney — a legacy of the city's

ery mixed population. For
Greek food, try the **Hellenic
Club,** 5th floor, 251 Elizabeth
treet, City (tel: 264 5883), which
s licensed and open for lunch
Monday to Friday; dinner
Monday to Saturday. A similar
establishment which specialises
n Spanish food is the **Spanish
Club,** 88 Liverpool Street, City
tel: 267 8630). The upstairs
restaurant serves traditional
Spanish fare daily for both lunch
and dinner and is licensed. For
general mid-European food, the
Gelato Bar, at 140 Campbell
Parade, Bondi Beach (tel: 30
4033) has stroganoff and exotica
such as Hungarian scrambled
eggs, in addition to gelato, cakes
and pastries. It is good value and
great food; BYO and open Tuesday to Sunday for lunch and
dinner. The cafés in Double Bay
serve the same kind of food with
a Jewish/mid European flair.

*The style of this Italian restaurant in
Paddington will be familiar to most*

French/International
Some of Sydney's finest (and
most expensive) restaurants
serve traditional and nouvelle
French food. **Claude's,** at 10
Oxford Street, Woollahra (tel:
331 2325) has an excellent
reputation and offers a fixed
price menu. It is BYO and opens
for dinner only from Tuesday to
Saturday. **Oasis Seros,** 495
Oxford Street, Paddington (tel:
33 3377) specialises in French
food with an oriental twist;
licensed and open for dinner
Tuesday to Sunday, lunch only
on Fridays. **Le Trianon,** 29
Challis Avenue, Potts Point (tel:
358 1353) offers modern
nouvelle style French food in an
elegant old terraced house;
licensed and serves dinner only
from Monday to Saturday.

Italian
Sydney's large Italian population
has brought a welcome host of
excellent restaurants in all price
categories. In the upper price

FOOD AND DRINK

range, two stand out: **Taylor's** at 203 Albion Street, Surry Hills (tel: 33 5100) presents northern Italian food at lunchtime on Fridays and for dinner Tuesday to Saturday, licensed; **Tre Scalini,** 174 Liverpool Street, East Sydney (tel: 331 4358) serves great seafood and pasta and is open for lunch and dinner on weekdays, dinner only on Saturday, licensed.

In the lower price range there is a bewildering choice. In the super-cheap bracket, the Stanley Street area of East Sydney has many cafés and restaurants, two of the most popular being **Bill and Toni's,** 72 Stanley Street (tel: 360 4702) and **No Name's,** 81 Stanley Street. Both are BYO and open for lunch and dinner daily, neither takes bookings and both have excellent coffee shops in addition to the upstairs restaurants. Two of the more expensive are the **Atlanta,** 41 Crown Street, Woolloomooloo (tel: 33 6467) which is open for lunch Monday to Friday and dinner Monday to Saturday, licensed; and **Russo** at 200 Crown Street, East Sydney, which is both BYO and licensed and is open Monday to Friday for lunch and Monday to Saturday for dinner. Mention must also be made of **Rossini,** which has two restaurants in the central city operating on a cafeteria style set-up and serving good cheap food, as well as just drinks for the non-diner: the Circular Quay restaurant has outdoor tables which look out on the harbour and is open daily from 07.00-20.00hrs (tel: 27 8026), while the Qantas International Centre Rossini (corner George and Jamison Streets, tel: 27 5894) is open for lunch Monday to Friday. Both are licensed.

'Oz Nouveau'

This innovative cuisine has made a big impact on the Sydney dining scene. Its lightness and freshness suits the climate, and the use of herbs, unusual flavourings and combinations of ingredients have revolutionised the basic meat and seafood dishes with which we are familiar. There are some excellent restaurants in this category, including the multi-award winning (and expensive) **Berowra Waters Inn,** Sydney's very top restaurant. Located at Berowra Waters (tel: 456 1017), north of the city, it is reached either by car and ferry or by seaplane from the city's Rose Bay. It is licensed and open for lunch and dinner, Friday to Sunday. **Kable's** at the Regent of Sydney hotel, 199 George Street (tel: 238 0000), is also classy and expensive; licensed and open Monday to Friday for lunch and dinner, Saturday and Sunday for dinner only.

More modestly, **Café Jax** at 64 Kellett Street, Kings Cross (tel: 357 2474) specialises in unusual pasta dishes and is popular with a young and trendy crowd; licensed and serves lunch and dinner daily. The **Paddington Inn Bistro** is located in a pub (388 Oxford Street, tel: 357 5913) and serves great food in unusual and brightly coloured surroundings. Licensed and open for lunch and dinner from

Although expensive, Doyles — famous for its seafood — is an institution on the lively Sydney restaurant scene

Tuesday to Sunday. Another excellent pub dining room is the **Four In Hand,** 105 Sutherland Street, Paddington (tel: 326 2254); here Oz Nouveau has an Italian twist. The restaurant is licensed and open for lunch and dinner daily.

Seafood

Sydney is justifiably famous for its incredible selection of seafood, with many varieties of fish, prawns, lobster, oysters, octopus and other local specialities. Char-grilled seafood is very popular, and something that the visitor should sample. One of Sydney's best seafood establishments also has a wonderful location overlooking Bondi Beach: the **Bluewater Grill,** 168 Ramsgate Avenue (tel: 30 7810), which has a large outdoor eating area. It is licensed and open for lunch

and dinner daily. **Doyles** at 11 Marine Parade, Watsons Bay (tel: 337 2007) is famous for its seafood and great view across the harbour, and there is now another Doyles at the Overseas Passenger Terminal at Circular Quay West. Both restaurants are licensed. The **Last Aussie Fishcaf** is a rock and roll café, complete with original Wurlitzer jukebox, which serves great seafood in a crazy atmosphere. It is at 24 Bayswater Road, Kings Cross (tel: 356 2911), is licensed and opens from lunch till late daily. For a more basic, pub-style taste of seafood, the **Woolloomooloo Bay Hotel** at 2 Bourke Street, Woolloomooloo is cheap and fun; licensed and open daily for lunch only. At night live music and large crowds take over.

Tourist Restaurants

More famous for their location and style than innovative food, these 'tourist' style restaurants

Co-operation in a country pub

are popular with visitors. Two with stunning views of the city are the **Summit Restaurant,** at the top of Australia Square Tower, George Street, City (tel: 27 9777), and **Sydney Tower Restaurant,** at the top of Sydney Tower, Centrepoint, City (tel: 233 3722). Both restaurants revolve and are worth visiting, especially for the night-time view. The **John Cadman Cruising Restaurant** (tel: 922 1922) cruises the harbour nightly at 19.30hrs and is another great way to dine and enjoy Sydney's wonderful views.

For further information on where to eat in Sydney call the Tourist Information Service on 669 5111.

Where to Drink

Drinking is a pretty serious business in Sydney, with the old standby location being one of the hundreds of Sydney hotels or pubs. Many are still very basic — simple watering holes with no frills — while,

particularly in the City and Paddington areas, others have been renovated to include dining rooms. As far as bars go, some of the best of these are to be found in the big hotels — more expensive, but the compensations are the pleasant surroundings, and the fact that they are often open much later than pubs. Other bars which have become popular are American-style cocktail bars which also serve food and often provide entertainment. All pubs and bars serve the normal spirits, beers and wines, including a range of Australia's excellent red and white wines. It is best to buy wine by the bottle, otherwise you will often be served 'chateau cardboard', wine from a cask, which is not the best on offer. Sydney's watering holes offer an incredible range of beers, many of which are from 'boutique' breweries, with a trend away from lagers and back to the more solid English-style beers. There are dozens to experiment with! Beer is served in middies (small glasses) and schooners (large), and by the bottle.

Pubs

Sydney's pubs are licensed to trade for 12 hours a day. Some are early openers, but most start business around 11.00hrs and trade through to 23.00hrs. Many hotels provide entertainment in the form of live music. You must be 18 or over to drink in a pub and most are not suitable places to take children, except for those with a beer garden or outdoor drinking area.

The Rocks area has two of the city's most interesting and historic pubs: the **Hero of Waterloo,** 81 Windmill Street, Millers Point (licensed since 1845 and very atmospheric), and the **Lord Nelson,** 19 Kent Street, Millers Point. This is Sydney's oldest hotel, built in 1834 and licensed since 1844. It has specially brewed beers and an upstairs dining room. In the city's Chinatown area and near to Darling Harbour, the **Pumphouse Brewery Tavern** at 17 Little Pier Street is one of the new boutique pubs which serves great beers and is located in an old pumping station. At Kings Cross, the **Oz Rock** at the corner of Victoria and William Streets is very popular with the younger crowd and gets incredibly crowded late at night.

Some of the best renovated hotels are in the inner east areas of Paddington and Woollahra. Here is the **Lord Dudley,** 236 Jersey Road, Woollahra, an English-style pub serving beer in pint and half-pint mugs and attracting a well-heeled, trendy crowd. There is a good courtyard restaurant downstairs. In Surry Hills, the **Cricketers Arms** at 106 Fitzroy Street, **The Brewers,** 354 Bourke Street, Darlinghurst, the **Dolphin** at 412 Crown Street, and the **Forresters Hotel** at 336 Riley Street, are all worth a visit, and most serve good food too. Over on the north shore, one of the most popular pubs is the **Oaks Hotel** at 118 Military Road, Neutral Bay, which is very large and extremely busy. Two waterside pubs are the **Hotel Bondi,** 178 Campbell Parade, Bondi Beach, and the **Watsons Bay Hotel,** 1 Military Road, Watsons Bay. Both are great for a summer outdoor drinking session.

Hotel Bars

For those more interested in sophistication and the accompanying higher prices, all of the big hotels have pleasant bars which stay open late and serve cocktails as well as regular drinks. The **Inter-Continental** at 117 Macquarie Street, City, has four bars, including the 31st floor Treasury Bar which has wonderful views of the city. Other city hotels with recommended bars are: The **Regent of Sydney,** 199 George Street; the **Sheraton Wentworth,** 61 Phillip Street; and the **Sydney Hilton International** at 259 Pitt Street. The latter has a wonderful bar and night club in

FOOD AND DRINK

its downstairs Marble Bar. In the Kings Cross area, the **Sebel Town House** has a small and intimate ground floor cocktail bar, and the **Sheraton Motor Inn** is famous for Jo Jo Ivory's restaurant and bar.

Cocktail and Wine Bars

Most of these establishments are connected to restaurants, so it is possible to both eat and drink under one roof. In terms of price they fall somewhere between pubs and hotel bars, and many offer happy hour prices in the early evening period.

In Kings Cross, **Barons** at 5 Roslyn Street, is above a restaurant and serves wine and cocktails till late in a relaxed atmosphere. The nearby **Bourbon and Beefsteak Bar** (24 Darlinghurst Road) is an American-style bar and restaurant which never seems to close. **Kinselas** is an old funeral parlour at 383 Bourke Street, Darlinghurst, which has a bar, restaurant and night club and is very popular with the trendy eastern suburbs set. In the city area there are several good bars of this type. **Charlie Brown's** at 90 Pitt Street is a wine bar which is popular with the after work city office crowd, and **Bobby McGee's** at the Festival Marketplace, Darling Harbour, is lively. The **Hard Rock Café** at 121 Crown Street, East Sydney, has good food and drink, but is loud.

Coffee Shops and Tearooms

If you are more interested in afternoon tea or a shot of strong Italian coffee there are plenty of cafés in the inner city and nearby areas, and all of the major tourist sites provide similar facilities. For really good coffee shops the Stanley Street area of East Sydney and Victoria Street, Darlinghurst, have some wonderful Italian establishments which serve cappuccino, black coffee, Italian soft drinks, cakes and pastries, and focaccia (Italian-style sandwiches). Some of the best are **Coluzzi Bar, Andiamo** and **Bar Michelangelo** in the Victoria Street region, and **Bill and Toni's** and **The Arch Coffee Shop** in Stanley Street. There are also some good cafés in the city centre. Some of the nicest teashops are located in museums, historic houses and art galleries: the **National Trust Centre** on Observatory Hill, The Rocks, **Juniper Hall** at 248 Oxford Street, Paddington, and the **Art Gallery of New South Wales** in the Domain all serve tea, coffee and good afternoon teas. Paddington's Oxford Street has several recommended cafés: try the **New Edition Tea Rooms** at 328a Oxford Street, which is also a bookshop, and **Cappuccino City,** opposite the Academy Twin Cinema at 12 Oxford Street.

Wine Tasting

If you would like to sample a range of the best Australian wines (with a view to buying), **Tastings at the Rocks,** 45 Argyle Street, The Rocks (tel: 241 3239) is open daily and offers wine tastings for groups or individuals, duty-free wine packs and a world wide delivery service — all in the pleasant atmosphere of an old Georgian house and courtyard.

SHOPPING

As Sydney is not particularly noted for its stunning fashions, other than in beach and casual wear, or for particularly cheap prices, most visitors head for those shops which sell distinctively Australian items. There is much to choose from. Australia has made the T-shirt and associated casual clothing a veritable art form, with well-known designers such as Ken Done and the Weiss Company producing high quality Australian theme designs on shorts, beach towels, mugs, sweatshirts and a host of other items. Aboriginal designs, too, have become very popular, both in genuine art and crafts, and in the clothing and souvenir industries. Traditional bushmen's clothing is another good buy: moleskin trousers, Akubra hats, Drizabone oilskin coats and bush shirts have

The Queen Victoria Building, elegantly and attractively restored from the 1898 vegetable market, is now a well-heeled shopper's dream

SHOPPING

become fashionable, and are hard wearing and practical too. Other items which interest the visitor are the famous Australian opal, sheepskin products and books on Australian history and culture. High quality wines are also popular shopping items.

The Main Areas

The main city shopping area stretches from The Rocks to Central Station and, east to west, from Elizabeth to George Streets. This area contains the major department stores, bookstores and a large number of shopping galleries and arcades. This is the area where the average Sydneysider buys clothes, household items, shoes, records, food — all the normal items. For the tourist, the best souvenir and gift shopping areas are The Rocks, Darling Harbour, Queen Victoria Building and Paddington's Oxford Street.

Saturday). Food and produce.
Glebe Market, corner Glebe
Point Road and Derby Street
(penultimate Saturday of each
month).
Kirribilli Market, Kirribilli
Neighbourhood Centre, Fitzroy
Street (last Saturday of each
month).
Paddington Market, Village
Church, Oxford Street,
Paddington (each Saturday,
10.00-17.00hrs). The biggest and
best of the local markets, which
sells an incredible variety of
goods and is worth visiting as
much for people-watching as
shopping.
Paddy's Market, next to Redfern
Railway Station (every Saturday
and Sunday). A large market
which sells everything from fruit
and vegetables to clothing,
records, handicrafts and pets.
Sydney Fish Market, corner
Gipps and Jones Streets, Pyrmont
(open daily). Amazing variety of
seafood.

Shopping and Fashion Tours
The really dedicated shopper
and bargain hunter can join a
variety of organised shopping
tours which obtain large dis-
counts from wholesalers and
manufacturers. Most of these
organisations concentrate on
fashion and clothing. Bargain
Buyer's Tours (tel: 440 8462/449
7221), Fashion Frolic (tel: 798
6755), Shopping Around (tel: 438
4248).

Antiques
The Paddington and Woollahra
areas are full of antique shops
and galleries, including these
two large centres which sell
anything from furniture to old
coins and jewellery:

You never know what you may find in a Saturday in Paddington Market

Markets
Saturday is the usual day for
browsing through crafts,
clothing, books and bric-a-brac
t one of Sydney's many
markets.
Balmain Market, St Andrews
Church, Darling Street, Balmain
Saturdays, from 07.30-16.00hrs).
Flemington Market, Parramatta
Road, Homebush (Friday and

SHOPPING

Sydney Antique Centre, 531 South Dowling Street, Surry Hills, (open every day from 10.30-18.00hrs).
Woollahra Galleries, 160 Oxford Street, Woollahra.

Duty Free Goods

Sydney has a highly competitive duty free trade, leading to some extremely low prices for many photographic, electrical and electronic goods, as well as perfumes, liquor, cigarettes, film, watches and jewellery. Prices for some items are lower than in Asian ports such as Hong Kong and Singapore, and overseas visitors are also entitled to tax free prices on Australian goods such as opals. You must produce your passport and air ticket in order to buy duty or tax free goods, and duty free items may not be collected until 48 hours prior to your departure from Australia. There are many reputable duty free stores in the city — check the yellow pages directory, or ask at your hotel. It is also possible to buy such goods at the airport before departure, but city prices are much cheaper. Inbound travellers can also buy duty free on arrival at Sydney Airport.

Australiana

Most of the suggestions below fall into the category of special interest items of Australiana, as these are the most worthwhile purchases for a visitor to Sydney.

Aboriginal art and artefacts:
Aboriginal-made paintings, carvings, boomerangs, baskets and fabrics make the most unusual and interesting gifts and souvenirs, and some are now highly regarded by the art world. Paintings can be very expensive, but smaller items should appeal to most tourists. The following shops sell authentic work:
Aboriginal Artists Gallery, 477 Kent Street, City.
Aboriginal Art Centre, Walker Lane, Paddington.
Bindi Gallery, Victoria Walk, Queen Victoria Building, George Street, City.

Australian art: Contemporary Australian art is exhibited and sold by many private galleries, particularly in the Paddington/Woollahra and Balmain areas, as well as the city. A couple of suggestions:
The Art Directors' Gallery (Ken Done's work), 21 Nurses Walk, The Rocks.
Holdsworth Galleries, 86 Holdsworth Street, Woollahra.

Australian clothing: The following shops specialise in Australian bush and outback clothing — the equivalent of the American cowboy look — including traditional Drizabone coats, Akubra hats (such as worn by golfer Greg Norman), riding boots, moleskin trousers and leather goods.
Morrisons, 105 George Street, The Rocks and Shop 135, Festival Marketplace, Darling Harbour.
R M Williams, 71 Castlereagh Street, City.
Strand Hatters, Shop 8, Strand Arcade, City.
Thomas Cook, 709 George Street, City.

Australian designers: Innovative knitwear and fashion clothing, often with an Australian theme,

Martin Place (or Plaza) is a huge shopping and entertainment area

is of good quality and has become very popular with visitors to Sydney. The following are recommended:
Bonz (hand-knits), Argyle Centre, The Rocks.
Coo-ee Australian Emporium (clothing and Aboriginal fabrics), 98 Oxford Street, Paddington and Shop 16, Strand Arcade, City.
Dorian Scott (hand-knits), 105 George Street, The Rocks.
Flamingo Park (clothing), Shop 102, Strand Arcade, City.
Ken Done (t-shirts, beachwear and other items), 123 George Street, The Rocks and Festival Marketplace, Darling Harbour.
Liz Newman's Designer Knits (hand-knits), Albert Walk, Queen Victoria Building, City.
Weiss Art (t-shirts, swimwear and other items), 85 George Street, The Rocks and Shop 475, Festival Marketplace, Darling Harbour.
Australian music: If Aboriginal and bush or folk music interests you, the best selection of tapes, records, CDs and songbooks

SHOPPING

is to be found at:
Folkways Music, 282 Oxford Street, Paddington.

Australian produce and wines:
Typically Australian foodstuffs such as macadamia nuts, cheeses, hand-made chocolates and award-winning wines and ports can all be bought all over Sydney, but the best selection is to be found at the David Jones Food Hall, Sydney's modest answer to Harrods or Fortnum and Mason: lower ground floor, David Jones, corner of Market and Castlereagh Streets, City. Sydney Airport has an Australian Produce Shop, which sells Australian cheeses, prawns, lobsters and other seafoods, meats, chocolates, wines, etc. Items are carefully packed to guarantee freshness during your flight home. Goods are duty free and are collected at the airport prior to departure (tel: 669 2740 or 667 3981 for details).

Crafts: For the best in contemporary Australian weaving, pottery, jewellery, leatherwork and many other crafts, visit the Crafts Council Gallery, 100 George Street, The Rocks, and Australian Craftworks, 127 George Street, The Rocks.

Gifts and souvenirs: There is a great deal of tacky rubbish in this category. The following shops sell good quality and often inventive Australian gifts and souvenirs; items such as Australian artist notelets, pot pourri, eucalyptus oil products and even Australia-shaped ice cube trays! Australian Museum Gift Shop, 6-8 College Street, City.
Best of Australiana, The Grand Walk, Queen Victoria Building, City.

Everything Australian, Harbourside Festival Marketplace, Darling Harbour and Clocktower Square, Argyle Street, The Rocks.
National Trust Gift Shops at Level 2, Queen Victoria Building, City; Clocktower Square, Argyle Street, The Rocks; and Juniper Hall, 248 Oxford Street, Paddington.
Wattle Tree Shop, 294 Oxford Street, Paddington.

Opals: Although not to everyone's taste, Australian opals are justifiably famous for their fine quality. These stones are composed of minute particles of silica and vary dramatically in colour; no two are alike. Opals are tax free to visitors, so take your passport and airline ticket with you. The following outlets can be recommended:
Gemtec Australia, 1st floor, 50 Park Street, City.
Gerrards Jewellers, 154 Castlereagh Street, City (Gerrards also specialise in diamonds from Western Australia's Argyle mine).
Opal Fields, Shop 191, Festival Marketplace, Darling Harbour.
Percy Marks, 65 Castlereagh Street, City.

Sheepskin products: Another distinctive and reasonably priced Australian product, which comes in the form of rugs, wall-hangings, toys, coats and other clothing. Available from:
Ausfurs, Clocktower Square, Argyle Street, The Rocks.
Aussie Ewe and Lamb, Argyle Centre, The Rocks.
Lambswool Trader, Metcalfe Arcade, 80 George Street, The Rocks.

Typical self-catering apartments in a south Sydney suburb

ACCOMMODATION

There is a wide variety of accommodation to suit all tastes and budgets, from top international standard hotels to dozens of backpackers' lodges. Serviced apartments, homestay and boutique guesthouses are also popular with tourists. There is no nationwide classification for hotels, but the suggestions which follow are divided into price categories — generally, you will get what you pay for. Making a reservation in advance is not usually a problem, but during the Christmas and January peak period rooms are often at a premium.

As a 'hotel' in Australia is also a pub, differentiating between watering holes with a few rooms upstairs, and a genuine tourist type hotel can sometimes be difficult. In this selection of accommodation, only a few establishments in the Economy category are pubs, chosen for their charm and appeal. For the same reason, Australians often refer to hotels as motels. All of the suggestions given are within easy reach of the city centre. If you are looking for a full list of hotels which covers all suburbs, contact the Australian Tourism Commission office nearest to you (see page 123). As far as meals are concerned, the more expensive hotels generally offer a room-only price, with breakfast being an additional cost, while smaller hotels usually include breakfast in the room charge. Serviced units and motels do not provide breakfast. If you haven't planned ahead, accommodation can be booked on arrival through the Airport Travellers' Information Service, which is located just outside the airport's arrival area.

Hotels

Deluxe

Considered by many to be the city's best hotel, the **Regent of Sydney** at 199 George Street (tel: 238 0000), just around the corner from The Rocks and Circular Quay, is the last word in luxury. The modern building occupies a prime site with superb harbour and city views, and the hotel contains excellent restaurants and facilities. The **Inter-Continental** at 117 Macquarie Street (tel: 230 0200) is another top class hotel. The lower levels occupy a beautiful old sandstone government building, the centrepiece of which is a lounge surrounded by arched, layered sandstone terraces; there is a wonderful city view from the top floor bar and restaurant. Also in the city centre, the **Sheraton-Wentworth** 61 Phillip Street (tel: 230 0700), is another classy establishment,

The luxury Inter-Continental Hotel: harbour views and gourmet dining

s are the **Holiday Inn Menzies,** 4 Carrington Street (tel: 20232) and the **Hilton International Sydney.** The latter was one of the city's earliest high-rise buildings and has some excellent bar and lounge areas. It is located at 259 Pitt Street (tel: 266 0610). Just out of the city centre, between the CBD and Kings Cross, **The Sydney Boulevard** at 90 William Street (tel: 357 2277) is another fine hotel. The 25th floor restaurant and nightclub afford wonderful views of the harbour and city. Sydney's most intimate top class hotel is the **Sebel Town House at Sydney** at 23 Elizabeth Bay Road, Elizabeth Bay (tel: 358 3244), just around the corner from Kings Cross. The Sebel is particularly popular with the rich and famous and is a member of the Leading Hotels of the World group.

Premier
In the city area, the **Wynyard Travelodge** at 7-9 York Street (tel: 29254) is near to Circular Quay and the business area, and offers good service and facilities. At the other end of town, in the Hyde Park region, the **Southern Cross,** corner of Elizabeth and Goulburn Streets, (tel: 20987), is popular with business travellers. The most stylish city hotel in this range is the **Old Sydney Parkroyal** on the corner of George Street and Mill Lane, The Rocks (tel: 20524). Built in the shell of an old warehouse, it is right in the centre of the fascinating Rocks area.
The inner eastern suburbs of Kings Cross, Potts Point and

Double Bay are convenient locations which have some excellent hotels. The **Hyatt Kingsgate,** Kings Cross Road, Kings Cross (tel: 357 2233) is an international standard hotel right in the heart of Sydney's nightlife area. Just across the road, the **Top of the Town** at 227 Victoria Street (tel: 33 0911) is somewhat more economical but has good facilities such as an outdoor pool and health club. The **Olims Sydney Hotel** at 26-34 Macleay Street, Potts Point (tel: 358 2777) is just outside the main Kings Cross area and most of its rooms have excellent harbour views. A little further east, but still very convenient, is the **Savoy Double Bay Hotel** (41-45 Knox Street, Double Bay, tel: 326 1411), a small boutique hotel. The North Shore area, just a few minutes away from the central city area and over the Harbour Bridge, has some excellent hotels for those needing to stay in this part of town. The **North Sydney Travelodge,** 17 Blue Street (tel: 92 0499) and **Noah's Northside Gardens** at 54 McLaren Street (tel: 922 1311) are both in the heart of the North Sydney business district. The seaside suburb of Manly — a pleasant ferry ride across the harbour — has the high quality **Manly Pacific Park Royal,** 55 North Steyne (tel: 977 7666), for those who like to stay in a quiet, out of town area.
Another excellent hotel in this category is the **Parramatta Parkroyal,** 30 Phillip Street (tel: 689 3333). Although 15 miles (24km) west of the city, this is **the** place to stay if you are seeing the Parramatta historic

ACCOMMODATION

sights or other parts of the city's western areas.

Moderate

This category has by far the largest number of hotels, many of which are motel-style (rooms have self-contained cooking facilities).

Two of the more expensive in this range are in the Kings Cross area and are both hotel rather than motel style. The **Gazebo Ramada**, 2 Elizabeth Bay Road, Elizabeth Bay (tel: 358 1999) is very convenient for transport and shops, as is the **Sheraton Hotel**, 40 Macleay Street, Potts Point (tel: 358 1955), which offers good facilities and the excellent Jo Jo Ivory's night club. Other establishments in this area include the **Clairmont Inn**, 5 Ward Avenue (tel: 358 2044), the **Metro Plainsman Motor Inn**, 40 Bayswater Road (tel: 356 3511), and the **Carnarvon Lodge**, 16 Ward Avenue (tel: 358 6611).

In the Hyde Park/Oxford Street area, the **Cambridge Inn**, 212 Riley Street, Darlinghurst (tel: 212 1111), **Koala Park Regis**, corner Park and Castlereagh Streets (tel: 267 6511) and the **Greetings Oxford Koala**, corner Oxford and Pelican Streets, Darlinghurst (tel: 269 0645) are all more than adequate, and are just a few minutes' walk from the city centre. Also in the inner east are the **Greetings Paddington Gardens**, 21 Oxford Street (tel: 360 2333), just a short bus ride from the city, and the **Greetings Motel Bondi Junction**, 79-85 Oxford Street (tel: 389 9466), ten minutes by train from Sydney's Martin Place.

Budget

Central city area: the **Grand Hotel**, 30 Hunter Street (tel: 232 3755), **George Street Private Hotel** at 700a George Street (tel: 211 1800), and the **Sydney Tourist Hotel**, 400 Pitt Street (tel: 211 5777) are all popular with lower-budget tourists. The Kings Cross area also has several similar hotels, including the **Challis Lodge**, 21-23 Challis Avenue, Potts Point (tel: 358 5422), the **Manhattan Hotel** at 8 Greenknowe Avenue, Potts Point (tel: 358 1288), and **Springfield Lodge**, 9 Springfield Avenue, Kings Cross (tel: 358 3222). Bondi Beach is also a good place to stay, particularly in summer. **Hotel Bondi**, corner Campbell Parade and Curlewis Street (tel: 30 3271) and the **Thelellen Beach Inn** at 2 Campbell Parade (tel: 30 5333) are both right on the main road, just off the beach.

Youth Hostels (A\$12 to A\$20 per person/per night)

The inner Sydney area has five youth hostels, all of which are located in the inner west or southern suburbs. They all aim to provide low cost accommodation and a friendly international atmosphere. In the beachside suburb of Coogee, the **Coogee YHA Hostel** at 102 Moverly Road (tel: 349 5355) is a great spot for those interested in beach life. The other YHA establishments are all around the University of Sydney region of Glebe, or further south; **Dulwich Hill YHA Hostel**, at 407 Marrickville Road (tel: 569 0271) is the most southerly. Those around Glebe are: **Forest Lodge**

HA Hostel, 28 Ross Street (tel: 92 0747), **Glebe Point YHA ostel**, 262-264 Glebe Point oad (tel: 692 8418), and the ew **Hereford YHA Lodge**, 52 ereford Street (tel: 660 5274). ontact the YHA, 176 Day Street el: 267 3044) for details of ostels within the outer Sydney egion.

ackpackers' Lodges

ydney's backpacker and young aveller's land is located in the ings Cross area, particularly in nd around Victoria Street, Potts oint. Most of the following rovide dormitory style ccommodation, as well as win-share private rooms. **ackpackers**, 162 Victoria treet, Potts Point (tel: 356 3232) s one of the original budget odges. Others in the same ocality are: **Down Under Hostel,** 5 Hughes Street, Kings Cross tel: 358 1143); **Jolly Swagman ackpackers**, 144 Victoria Street tel: 358 6400); **Plane Tree odge**, 172 Victoria Street (tel: 56 4551); and **Travellers' Rest,** 56 Victoria Street (tel: 358 606). The new **Backpackers leadquarters** chain has five odges, four of which are in the Kings Cross area: 79 Bayswater Road, Kings Cross (tel: 331 2520), 59 Bayswater Road (tel: 332 3284), 6-8 Orwell Street (tel: 358 2185) and also at 164 Bourke Street, Darlinghurst (tel: 331 5245). In the central city area, **ydney City Centre ackpackers**, at 7 Elizabeth Street (tel: 223 3629), provides he same sort of accommodation. In other parts of the inner suburbs, **Coogee ackpackers**, 94 Beach Street,

Sydney has a big range of budget accommodation to cater for the large number of backpackers and young travellers who visit the city each year

Coogee (tel: 665 7735), and another **Backpackers Headquarters,** at 243 Cleveland Street, Central (tel: 698 8839), are good value at a slightly further distance from the city.

Boutique Hotels and Guesthouses

Prices vary considerably, but all include continental breakfast. **The Russell,** at 143a George Street, The Rocks (tel: 241 3543) is an 18-room hotel located in an 1887 building. All rooms are tastefully decorated in Victorian style. Similar establishments are found in the Kings Cross area: **The Kendall,** 122 Victoria Street, Potts Point (tel: 357 3200), **The**

ACCOMMODATION

Jackson, 84 Victoria Street, Potts Point (tel: 358 5144), and **Simpsons of Potts Point,** 8 Challis Avenue (tel: 356 2199). All of these guesthouses occupy old buildings, and the latter is a recently restored 1892 mansion. **Waratah House,** at 108 Oxford Street, Darlinghurst (tel: 332 4118) is close to the city. In the inner west, **Pensione Sydney** at 25-27 Georgina Street, Newtown (tel: 550 1700) and **Newington Manor,** 10-14 Sebastopol Street, Stanmore (tel: 560 4289) are both old buildings which have been restored for guesthouse use. Over the bridge, in the charming suburb of Kirribilli, the **Kirribilli Bed and Breakfast** at 12 Parkes Street (tel: 922 3134) runs the same kind of personalised show.

Serviced Apartments

Serviced apartments offer cooking facilities and are serviced daily, and are a more economical alternative to hotels for either families, or people travelling in groups. All of those listed below offer one or two bedrooms, and some have three. Many have swimming pools and other facilities. Prices vary considerably.
Central city area: **The Park Apartments,** 16-32 Oxford Street, Darlinghurst (tel: 331 7728); **Savoy Serviced Apartments,** corner King and Kent Streets, City (tel: 267 9211); **The York,** 5 York Street, City (tel: 264 7747); and **Waldorf Apartments,** 57 Liverpool Street, City (tel: 290 1200). **Sydney Visitors Apartments** have a range of eight different buildings in the inner city (tel:

290 1166). The Kings Cross area has several serviced apartment buildings: **Seventeen,** 17 Elizabeth Bay Road, Elizabeth Bay (tel: 358 8999) is expensive, others are the **Florida Motor Inn,** 1 McDonald Street, Potts Point (tel: 358 6811), and the **Merlin Plaza,** 2 Springfield Avenue, Potts Point (tel: 356 3255). Inner eastern suburbs: **Oakford White City,** overlooking the White City tennis club at 400 Glenmore Road, Paddington (tel: 332 3484); and **Stanford Executive Apartments,** 1 Hollywood Avenue, Bondi Junction (tel: 389 8700). Both are in the more expensive category. On the northside, try **Sydney Serviced Apartments,** 145/14 Blues Point Road, McMahons Point (tel: 923 2611), just across the Harbour Bridge from the city.

Bed and Breakfast/Homestay

Homestays are economical and are a good way to really get to know Sydneysiders. Sydney has several central booking agencies which have a wide variety of homes in different suburbs on their books, and these are listed below. Contact the agencies direct for brochures and information.
At Home Down Under, PO Box 98, Cremorne Junction, NSW 2090 (tel: (02) 960 4481).
Away From Home Accommodation, 41a Clissold Road, Wahroonga, NSW 2076 (tel: (02) 489 5653).
Bed and Breakfast Australia, PO Box Q184, Sydney, NSW 2001 (tel: (02) 264 3155).
Houseguest, PO Box 636, Spit Junction, NSW 2088 (tel: (02) 960 2047).

NIGHTLIFE

Sydney is not short of places to go after dark, and there is something for all tastes. For a supposedly 'uncultural' city there is a very good selection of ballet, opera, classical music concerts and mainstream theatre, while jazz, rock, cinema, fringe theatre, night clubs and gay bars are all much in evidence. The Central city area has most of the main cinemas, theatres and some night clubs, and of course the Opera House, where classical entertainment is performed. Kings Cross is pretty sleazy, but it is where all the real late night action happens. Here there are many restaurants, bars, clubs, sex and strip shows, and constant street life. The Cross's Darlinghurst Road is where it all happens and it is at its busiest on Friday and Saturday nights. Darlinghurst is also pretty lively, with most of the gay bars and clubs along the 'Great Gay Way', and many restaurants and discos or live music clubs. The Rocks area is full of pubs and restaurants and is good earlier in the evening; there is not much happening here after 23.00hrs.

Most of the city's nightspots are concentrated in the Kings Cross area

What's On

The best sources of entertainment information (for both day and night activities) is the *Sydney Morning Herald Metro Guide,* which is included in the Friday paper, and lists everything from rock concerts to art exhibitions. *The Herald* also has a comprehensive entertainment section in the Saturday paper. *City Life* magazine comes out each month and gives detailed information of events for the coming month. For rock music fans, *On the Street* is a weekly newspaper which is given away in pubs and at various other locations.

The magnificent Opera House gives the impression of being about to float away across the harbour

Tickets

The central ticket agency for all major theatrical, operatic, dance, sporting and concert events is Ticketek (tel: 260 4800). Cinema tickets are always bought direct from the relevant theatre. The Halftix booth in Martin Place sells reduced price tickets for all major events from 12 noon on the day of performance. It means queueing but is worthwhile if you are keen to see something in particular.

Where to Go

Classical Concerts, Ballet and Opera

The home of Sydney's mainstream entertainment is, not surprisingly, the Sydney Opera House, which contains a concert hall, opera theatre, drama theatre and playhouse. Productions by the Australian Opera, Australian Ballet, Sydney Symphony Orchestra, Sydney Philharmonia Choir and Sydney Theatre Company are all regular features, as well as appearances by visiting orchestras and soloists. Information on any Opera House event is available from the box office (tel: 250 7777).

Classical music concerts are also often performed at the Sydney Town Hall, and by music students at the NSW State Conservatorium of Music (tel: 230 1263).

Theatre

Theatre is alive and well in Sydney and some 20 venues are home to mainstream theatre, musicals and fringe, including big international productions like *Cats* and *Les Miserables,* and good Australian drama by playwrights such as David Williamson. Some of the major companies and theatres: **Belvoir Street Theatre,** 25 Belvoir Street, Surry Hills (tel: 699 3273) concentrates on mainstream plays with some cabaret productions. Over on the north shore, the **Ensemble Theatre** at 78 McDougall Street, Milsons Point (tel: 929 0644) puts on a mostly mainstream programme and is the north side's major theatre. City theatres include the **Theatre Royal** at the MLC Centre, King Street (tel: 231 6111) and **Her Majesty's Theatre,** 107 Quay Street (tel: 266 4800), both of which are large performance spaces where the big musicals and international shows are performed. **The Seymour Centre,** at the corner of City Road and Cleveland Street, City (tel: 692 3511) has three theatres which present a wide variety of shows, anything from conventional to innovative. The **Wharf Theatre** at Pier 4, Walsh Bay (tel: 250 1777) is home of the Sydney Theatre Company who often perform lesser-known and more experimental plays. Other theatre venues are the **Footbridge Theatre,** Parramatta Road, Broadway (tel: 692 9955), the **Stables Theatre** at 10 Nimrod Street, Kings Cross (tel: 33 3817), and the **Opera House Drama Theatre.**

Dance

Other than formal ballet at the Opera House, there are a couple of exciting dance companies who perform at various venues: the **Sydney Dance Company** (innovative), and the **Aboriginal and Islander Dance Theatre,** who are a unique group specialising in native Australian dance.

Cinema

Sydney's cinemas are mainly located in two city areas — Pitt Street between Market and Park Streets, and on George Street, between Bathurst and Liverpool. These theatres show all the major international and Australian movies, and the big chains such as Hoyts, Village and Greater Union also have cinemas in many suburban areas. Australia has four censorship categories: G=General exhibition; PG=Parental guidance; M=Mature audiences and R=Restricted to persons over 18. For all cinema programmes and starting times, refer to the *Sydney Morning Herald* or any daily paper.

In addition to the major cinemas there are some excellent independent theatres which show limited appeal selected releases, 'art' films and old movies. These include: **Academy Twin Cinema,** 3a Oxford Street, Paddington (tel: 33 4453); the **AFI** (Australian Film Institute Cinema) at Paddington Town Hall, corner of Oxford Street and Oatley Road (tel: 33 5398); **The Dendy,** MLC Centre, Martin Place, City (tel: 233 8166); the **Mandolin,** 150 Elizabeth Street, City (tel: 267 1968); and the **Valhalla,** at 166 Glebe Point Road, Glebe (tel: 660 8850).

The city's 1929 **State Theatre** in Market Street deserves a special mention for its wonderful, over-the-top décor. In addition to movies, it puts on concerts and musicals and is the venue for the annual Sydney Film Festival each June.

Jazz

Both traditional and contemporary jazz are big in Sydney. There are many popular bands and some good venues, and even a Jazz Hotline (tel: 818 5177) which you can call for details of who is appearing where and when. Among the most popular clubs are: **Blue Note Jazz Basement;** 147a King Street (tel: 221 4322), has bands every night of the week except Monday, and is open from 21.00-03.00hrs. The **Don Burrows Supper Club** at the Regent Hotel, 199 George Street (tel: 238 0000) is a sophisticated jazz and supper club in Sydney' best hotel; open from Tuesday to Saturday from 21.00hrs, it features the excellent Don Burrows Quintet and guest bands. **Soup Plus** at 383 George Street (tel: 29 7728) is a jazz venue with a difference. The restaurant serves delicious soups and meals to a jazz background, and it has a great, friendly atmosphere. Open Monday to Saturday, with jazz from 19.30-22.30hrs. Also in the city, the **Real Ale Café** not only serves good food and over 80 types of beers, its also has live jazz from Wednesday to Friday 20.00hrs to midnight; 66 King Street (tel: 262 3277). The **Richmond Riverboat** (tel: 27 2979) has evening and daytime jazz cruises on the harbour, complete with views and food. Two other good jazz spots are **Klub Kakadu,** 163 Oxford Street Darlinghurst (tel: 331 1140), with jazz, rock music and a disco; and **Round Midnight,** 2 Roslyn Street, Kings Cross (tel: 356 4045), a small and upmarket club, open daily from 20.00-03.00hrs.

Rock and Contemporary Music

The big international or Australian bands pack them in at large venues such as the Hordern Pavilion, Sydney Town

all, or more commonly, the
ast Sydney Entertainment
entre, but the popularity of live
ock has led to the
ushrooming of small venues all
ver the city. There are clubs of
l sizes and a great number of
ubs which provide live music
r their eager customers. Some
the most popular venues to

catch good local bands such as
The Cockroaches, Party Boys or
Gondwanaland, an Aboriginal
group, are: **Annandale Hotel,**
corner of Nelson Street and
Parramatta Road, Annandale
(tel: 51 2016), with bands on

*You will find a lot to do in the
Darling Harbour Complex, opened
for the Bicentennial in 1988*

Wednesday to Sunday from
18.30hrs; **Harold Park Hotel,** 115
Wigram Road, Glebe (tel: 692
0564), which has rock bands
most nights, as well as Writers
and Comics in the Park, comedy
and readings by contemporary
writers; the **Harbourside
Brasserie** (Pier One, Walsh Bay,
tel: 27 8222) also has rock on
some nights, as well as jazz
evenings. Other large venues
include the **Kardomah Café,** 22
Bayswater Road, Kings Cross
(tel: 358 522), with bands nightly
from 21.45hrs; **Selinas** at the
Coogee Bay Hotel, 253 Coogee
Bay Road, (tel: 665 0000);
Sydney Cove Tavern, Young
Street, Circular Quay (tel: 231
6099); and **St James
Underground Tavern,** 80
Castlereagh Street, City (tel: 221
2468): bands on Thursday nights
and a disco on Friday and

*There are many steakhouses,
brasseries, bistros and wine bars in
the Kings Cross area where it is
possible to eat well and reasonably*

Saturday. Other pub venues
include the **Golden Sheaf Hotel,**
429 South Head Road, Double
Bay (tel: 327 5877), bands on
Thursday to Sunday nights; the
Hopetoun Hotel, 416 Bourke
Street, Surry Hills (tel: 33 5257),
rock from Wednesday to
Sunday evenings; and the
Lansdowne Hotel, 2 City Road,
Broadway (tel: 211 2325),
Tuesday to Sunday from
20.00hrs. The **Woolloomooloo
Bay Hotel** (2 Bourke Street,
Woolloomooloo, tel: 357 1928)
features the terrific rock and
rollers, The Eddys, on Sunday
nights. It gets unbelievably
crowded but is a lot of fun.

Folk Music
This isn't very popular in
Sydney, but when it is on you
will find it on the pub scene —
check the entertainment guides
for details.

Discos and Nightclubs
If you are interested in being
the action, rather than watching
it, there are many dance and
disco clubs to suit all age
ranges and pockets. Most
nightclubs stay open till around
02.00 or 03.00hrs and many have
a cover charge which varies from
A$5 to A$20. Drink prices also
vary dramatically, according to
the club's level of sophistication.
In the upper price (and
generally age) range, the
following are popular: **Base,** at
11 Jamison Street, City (tel: 251
1480), very hi-tech and open,
with various themes on different
nights, from Tuesday to
Saturday, 22.00-03.00hrs; **The
Brink,** situated in the Hilton
Hotel's wonderful Marble Bar
(259 Pitt Street, City, tel: 266

At 'Les Girls' in Roslyn Street, Kings Cross, there is a long-established and extremely popular show featuring female impersonators

610), which is in operation from Monday to Saturday and has both live music and a disco; **The Cauldron,** 207 Darlinghurst Road, Darlinghurst (tel: 33 1152), which attracts a super-trendy crowd and is open nightly; and **Rogues,** 10 Oxford Square, Darlinghurst (tel: 33 6924). Here there is no cover charge, but you really have to look trendy and expensive to get in. Two hotel nightclubs which are expensive but glossy, are **Juliana's** at the Sydney Hilton, 259 Pitt Street, City (tel: 266 0610), open from Tuesday to Saturday and often features live

performances by visiting artists such as Randy Crawford; and **Williams** at the Boulevard Hotel, 90 William Street (tel: 357 2277). Others in the more upmarket range are the **Café Royale,** 36 Bayswater Road, Kings Cross (tel: 358 4528), open nightly from 17.00-03.00hrs; and **Kinselas,** Taylor Square, Darlinghurst (tel: 331 6200). This is an old funeral parlour which features live music, a disco, cocktail bar and restaurant, as well as cabaret shows. Open daily from 10.00-03.00hrs.
For the younger crowd there is also a good selection of places to bop the night away, and these are generally cheaper for both cover charge and drinks. In the central city area, the **Craig**

NIGHTLIFE

Brewery at Darling Harbour (tel: 281 3922) has both a disco and live music on some nights, and is open every night, and **St James Underground Tavern** at 80 Castlereagh Street (tel: 221 2468) is popular with a young age group who dance to either live bands or a disco. Over on the north shore, **Metropolis** at 99 Walker Street, North Sydney, is open Monday to Saturday and has a wide range of entertainment, including a disco, live music and a bistro. In the eastern suburbs there are several good venues: **The Freezer** at 11 Oxford Street, Paddington (tel: 332 2568) has different entertainment each night and is extremely popular; open Wednesday to Saturday from 21.00-03.00hrs, and on Sunday until 04.00hrs. **Klub Kakadu** at 163 Oxford Street, Darlinghurst (tel: 331 4001) also has a very varied range of activities, with an upstairs live venue and restaurant as well as a dance club; open from 18.00-03.00hrs Wednesday to Saturday. Nearby **Spago's** (238 Crown Street, Darlinghurst, tel: 331 5023) has a restaurant and a popular dance floor for the young and trendy.

Other Entertainment

Theatre Restaurants: Sydney is not known for entertainment of this type, but there are a couple of venues which might appeal: the Comedy Store Theatre at Margaret Lane (off Jamison Street, City, tel: 251 1480) provides dinner, drinks and laughs, while Les Girls, 2c Roslyn Street, Kings Cross (tel: 358 2333) is a long-standing and popular all male drag show.

The Gay Scene: Oxford Street is the home of Sydney's thriving gay scene. Here are numerous bars, clubs and pubs such as The Albury, 6 Oxford Street, Paddington, The Exchange, 34 Oxford Street, Darlinghurst, The Midnight Shift, 85 Oxford Street, Darlinghurst, and The Outpost at 182 Oxford Street, Paddington, which caters for both men and women.

Gambling: Australians are inveterate gamblers, and although Sydney has no casino, there are many illegal gambling dens, which are not recommended. Poker machines (pokies) are a more common outlet for the gambling urge, and many social and sporting clubs display ranks of these coin-eating monsters. If you're interested in this form of entertainment, try the Sydney Aussie Rules Club at 28 Darlinghurst Road, Kings Cross. If you want to place a bet on the horses, greyhounds or football, go to the nearest TAB (Totalizator Agency Board) office, which has outlets throughout the city.

Night Tours: several companies run 'Sydney by night' tours which are a good way to see different aspects of the city's nightlife. Contact AAT Kings (tel: 666 3899), Australian Pacific Tours (tel: 27 2721), Clipper Tours (tel: 888 3144) and Newmans Australia (tel: 231 6511).

Daytime Entertainment: There is often outdoor entertainment, which is free of charge, at venues like the Opera House, Darling Harbour and Martin Place.

WEATHER AND WHEN TO GO

Sydney has a warm, temperate, sunny climate with few extremes. Summer days can be hot and humid, with refreshing, cooler evenings, while the winter is rarely cold. Spring and autumn are mild and generally sunny. Most rain falls during March and June, with the coldest month being July and the hottest January/February. Thunderstorms are quite common in summer and sunshine is prevalent all year.

What to Bring

Australians are very informal in their dress, so visitors should bring smart casual clothes. Shorts are quite acceptable for both sexes and you should bring a light sweater or jacket for the occasional cool evening. A sunhat and sunglasses are on the essentials list for summer visits. In spring and autumn a raincoat and/or umbrella are suggested. Winters are relatively mild — gloves, warm hats or scarves are virtually never needed, but you should bring a warm jacket or coat and sweaters.

When to Go

Any time is a good time to visit Sydney, although the most popular time for northern hemisphere visitors is,

Although Sydney does not suffer extremes of temperature, forest fires can be a hazard at the height of summer

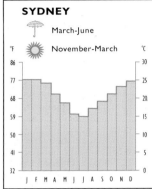

SYDNEY

☂ March-June

☀ November-March

°F		°C
86		30
77		25
68		20
59		15
50		10
41		5
32		0

J F M A M J J A S O N D

obviously, the Australian summer. The only drawbacks, especially in January, are that the city is full of visitors, and it is also school holiday time. Alternative times that still provide plenty of sunshine and good weather are October/ November and February/March. If you are planning to visit the outback and northern parts of the continent, summer is not the best time as temperatures reach 40°C (102°F)in many areas. Better to plan your trip for the April to September period.

HOW TO BE A LOCAL

There is a formula for impersonating Sydneysiders, but depending on what sort of person you are, it can be deceptively hard. The secret is to look relaxed, unbothered and somewhat *laissez faire,* wear casual clothes, and get a tan. Sydneysiders say 'g'day' instead of good morning, men call other men 'mate', as in 'excuse me, mate, have you got a light?', and most people say thanks instead

of please, which is actually quite economical. An example: a woman boards a bus and buys a ticket: 'one dollar, thanks'. In the same economical vein, Australians abbreviate every-thing. If your name is Gary, you'll become Gazza, and any-thing short will become familiar ised, as in Johnno for John. As far as habits are concerned, some visitors may be surprised or even shocked by the casualness of everything. Eating on the street is a national pastime, even with starchy businessmen. Beer drinking is an essential, preferably straight from the can or bottle if you really want to look the part. Drinking wine is OK for women. Walking around half dressed is *de rigeur* too. Don't be surprised to see girls in bikini tops and short shorts in the middle of the city in summer, or men wearing just a pair of shorts. As for beach life, we're looking at a lot less. If any of these habits shock you, just remember that Sydney was founded by convicts and that we've had only 200 years to get over the fact.

EVENTS

January
Festival of Sydney (includes Australia Day, 26 January)
Test cricket matches
New South Wales Open tennis

February
Chinese New Year celebrations
Gay Mardis Gras festival and parade

March
Golden Slipper horse race

*he Royal Easter Show, NSW's major
*gricultural exhibition

oyal Easter Show
*March/April)

pril
eritage Week
ustralian Motor Cycle Grand
<ix, Bathurst
/dney Cup horse race

lay — July
iennale Festival (in even
ears)

une
/dney Film Festival
SW ski season opens
oliday and travel show

ugust
ity to Surf fun run

September
Carnivale (1st two weeks)
Rugby Union Grand Final
Rugby League Grand Final
Mudgee wine festival

October
Australian indoor tennis
championships
Opera House open day and
pageant
Manly Jazz Festival
Bathurst 1000 saloon car race
Upper Hunter Valley wine
festival

December
Carols by Candlelight (at
various locations)
Sydney to Hobart yacht race
(26 December)

CHILDREN

CHILDREN

It is appropriate that a fresh new city such as Sydney offers much to entertain the young, and the young at heart! Most activities and venues for children will also appeal to adults, and this makes many ideal for family outings. Although there is much to do in the city itself, most of the theme and amusement parks are well outside the city centre, and it would be preferable to hire a car rather than rely on public transport.

Fun and Theme Parks

Australiana Park, Camden Valley Way, Narellan (near Campbelltown). Koalas, kangaroos, baby animals, waterslides, pony rides and boomerang-throwing are just some of this park's attractions. The day's highlight is a performance of the white Andalusian stallions in an indoor arena. Picnic and barbecue facilities are provided in addition to restaurants.
Open: 10.00-17.00hrs, daily
Train to Campbelltown, then a private bus to the park
Australiana Pioneer Village, Rose Street, Wilberforce (near Windsor). This re-creation of a colonial pioneer village feature original 19th-century buildings,

Sydney is a place for young people, and there are lots of funfairs all over the city, in addition to the huge theme parks

including Rose Cottage, built in 1811 and Australia's oldest timber dwelling still existing on its original site. The village aims to present a faithful picture of life in the early Sydney days and a visit will include demonstrations of sheep shearing, wool spinning and the blacksmith's art. Other attractions are rides on a horse-drawn vehicle, visiting the native animal enclosure, and afternoon tea with traditional damper and billy tea.

Open: 10.00-17.00hrs Tuesday to Thursday, Saturday and Sunday
Train to Windsor station and then a taxi

Australia's Wonderland, Wallgrove Road, Minchinbury (near Blacktown). The slogan here is 'too much fun to have in one day' and it is not surprising, with many amusement rides such as the Bush Beast rollercoaster and Bounty's Revenge, a giant swinging ship. The park also includes a theatre which gives five live song and dance or acrobatic shows daily; children's games and restaurant facilities.
Open: 10.00-21.00hrs Saturdays, 10.00-18.00hrs Sundays
Train to Mt Druitt, Fairfield, Rooty Hill or Blacktown and then a private shuttle bus

Old Sydney Town, Pacific Highway, Somersby (near Gosford). Another re-creation of life in a bygone age, this time of old Sydney itself. The set up includes historic buildings, street theatre, characters such as a town crier, soldiers or convicts undergoing a flogging; all in period dress. Several restaurants are on the site, as are picnic and barbecue facilities.
Open: 10.00-17.00hrs Wednesday to Sunday and public holidays
Train to Gosford and then a pick-up coach service

Zoos, Wildlife Parks and Aquariums

African Wildlife Safari, Warragamba Dam. This safari reserve, around one hour's drive west of Sydney, includes 80 lions, bears, tigers and other animals roaming free (feeding

at 14.00hrs each day); a dolphin and sealion show; pets corner, kangaroo reserve and children's rides and playground. It is worth visiting, especially if combined with a visit to nearby Warragamba Dam and Lake Burragorang, the main source of Sydney's water supply.
Open: from 10.00hrs Wednesday to Sunday and all public holidays
Drive or take a coach tour — contact The Travel Centre of New South Wales (tel: 231 4444)

Koala Park Sanctuary, Castle Hill Road, West Pennant Hills. Opened in 1930, this was NSW's first private koala sanctuary which conducts research and breeding programmes with the aim of preserving the endangered koala, one of Australia's unmistakable national symbols. In addition to the wonderful koalas (cuddling permitted), the 10 acre park contains dingoes, wallabies, possums, wombats, kangaroos and a wide variety of Australian birds. Picnic and barbecue facilities are provided.
Open: 09.00-17.00hrs daily
Train to Pennant Hills (via Strathfield) and bus number 655

Featherdale Wildlife Park, 217 Kildare Road, Doonside (near Blacktown).
Open: 09.00-17.00hrs daily
Train to Blacktown, then Leslies bus number 211

Waratah Park, Namba Road, Duffy's Forest. This includes a 60-minute adventure bushwalk.
Open: 10.00-17.00hrs daily
Train to Chatswood then Forest Coach Lines bus number 56

Sydney Aquarium, Pier 26, Darling Harbour. This well-planned new project is one of the many attractions at the city's Darling Harbour complex. The Aquarium features displays on Australian river systems, the Great Barrier Reef and crocodiles, as well as over 5,000 fish and reptiles, including sharks, rays, turtles and the marine life of Sydney Harbour. A 'touch pool' allows children to pick up marine creatures such as shellfish and sea urchins.
Open: 09.30-21.00hrs daily
Monorail from Pitt Street, or walk from the city centre

Taronga Zoo, Bradleys Head Road, Mosman. This is a must for all visitors, for, apart from the animal attractions, it must be the world's best sited zoo. Reached by a short ferry ride from Circular Quay, the zoological gardens are set on a hillside with a marvellous view of the harbour and city. The zoo focuses on Australia's unique animal, fish and birdlife but also includes animals and birds from every continent. Highlights are the seals, which perform daily; the 'animals of the night display' and, especially for kids, the Friendship Farm — the home of orphaned native animals. The cable car provides an excellent view of both zoo and city.
Open: 09.00-17.00hrs daily
Ferry from Circular Quay

Museums

Many of Sydney's museums hold a particular appeal for children. The Australian Museum has intriguing natural history and Aboriginal displays, while the Sydney Observatory's visitor-operated astronomy and physics

isplays will appeal to older
hildren and adults. The
ustralian Museum of
hildhood at Paddington's
uniper Hall will interest kids
o. Probably the best
hild-oriented museum though
the Powerhouse, where
quisitive kids of all ages will
e fascinated by the many fun,
ands-on displays. For full
etails of all these, see the What
See chapter.
he **Lego Centre,** Birkenhead
oint, Drummoyne. Although not
rictly a museum, all children
ill love this huge display of
ego work which includes over
0 models of objects such as
e Opera House, dinosaurs and
pacecraft. Kids can create their

own models and a full range of
Lego and Duplo sets are avail-
able for sale. Birkenhead Point
also offers shops, a market area,
marina and the Sydney Maritime
Museum for a full day out. The
ferry ride there is also fun.
Open: 09.30-17.00hrs daily
*Bus 500 or 502 from Circular
Quay*
Ferry from Circular Quay West

Other Activities
Check *City Life* monthly
magazine for details of
children's workshops, theatre
performances and other
activities.

TIGHT BUDGET

Sydney is not a bad place to be
if you are travelling with limited
means. For accommodation,
generally you are best off
heading for one of the city's five

*ecause wombats spend much of
eir time in burrows underground
d are mainly nocturnal, you are
likely to see them in the wild*

youth hostels, or the Victoria Street area of Kings Cross. The latter area is Sydney's backpackers' city, with many hostels, lodges, restaurants and notice boards advertising air tickets, items for sale and shared car travel for trips around Australia.

If you are planning to be in the city for any length of time it would be wise to purchase a copy of *Cheap Eats in Sydney*. For cheap Italian restaurants, head for east Sydney's Stanley Street, where you can have a bowl of pasta for under A$5. Govinda's, the Hare Krishna restaurant at 112 Darlinghurst Road, Darlinghurst, serves a vegetarian smorgasbord for A$5, while the New York in Kings Cross' Kellett Street dishes up meat and three veg style meals for around the same price. The YWCA cafeteria at 5 Wentworth Avenue, City serves excellent meals for between A$5 and A$7. For other cheap restaurants, try the Darlinghurst Road area between Kings Cross and Oxford Street, and Oxford Street around the Taylor Square area. There are also dozens of cheap snack bars around the city. As far as drinking is concerned, stick to the more colourful but basic Aussie hotels (pubs), where drinks cost considerably less.

Most Sydney museums and galleries do not charge entrance fees. The central area is small enough to walk around, and when you've had enough of history and culture, Sydney's parks, beaches and sunshine are all free of charge!

The Metroten, Day Rover and Sydneypass tickets all offer considerable savings on public transport. It is also cheaper to travel by train after 09.00hrs and to buy a return rather than single ticket. Use the harbour ferries instead of tour boats for your harbour sightseeing; the trip to Manly is particularly good value, half an hour's cruising for under A$2.

Sydney has several venues where free concerts are a regular feature. The Opera House forecourt on Sunday afternoons offers jazz, folk groups and, sometimes, ethnic dance groups; weekday lunchtimes at Martin Place's amphitheatre bring anything from brass bands to theatre; while Darling Harbour puts on a wide variety of entertainment on Saturdays and Sundays. Many movie theatres offer reduced price admission on Tuesdays, and if you want to see opera, ballet, theatre or any big sporting event, the Halftix booth at Martin Place (near Elizabeth Street) sells half price tickets on the day of performance, from 12 noon. You'll have to join the often long queue, but it is worth the effort.

SPECIAL INTEREST EXCURSIONS

Sydney has a wide choice of tour operators. Some suggestions are given below, but you should contact the Travel Centre of New South Wales for full details or to make bookings (tel: 231 4444).

Adventure tours. Adventure travel is very popular in Australia, and there is a large

SPECIAL INTEREST EXCURSIONS

An aerial view of Watsons Bay

number of operators in the Sydney area who provide thrills in the form of abseiling, rockclimbing, horseriding, canoeing, sea kayaking, bushwalking, cycling, diving, four wheel drive trips or fishing. All of these activities are available within a 125 mile (200km) radius of the city. In winter (June to September) the ski season operates in the Snowy Mountains in southern New South Wales.

Out and About (tel: (047) 84 2361)

Wild Escapes (tel: 660 2584)

World Expeditions (tel: 264 3366)

Air tours. A bird's eye view is one of the best ways to see Sydney's spectacular layout, and air tours include anything from cruising over the harbour in an airship, to a helicopter tour to the Hunter Valley wineries.

Airship Flights (tel: 234 4000) (or book through any Thomas Cook office)

Aquatic Airways (seaplane) (tel: 919 5966)

Heliflite (helicopters) (tel: 680 1511)

Kingsford Smith Air Tours (tel: 708 1133)

Red Baron Scenic Flights (tel: 771 1333) (Tiger Moth flights)

Sydney Aerial Tours (tel: 709 4953)

Sydney Helicopter Service (tel: 27 5151)

Coach tours. All operators run

SPECIAL INTEREST EXCURSIONS

similar itineraries.
AAT Kings (tel: 666 3899)
Australian Pacific Tours (tel: 27 2721)
Clipper Tours (tel: 888 3144)
Newmans Australia (tel: 225 8061)
Pioneer Trailways (tel: 387 3895)
Cruises and boat trips. This is another great way to see Sydney. Again, there are many operators, but the following are all recommended. All include meals or snacks during the cruise, and some provide entertainment also.
Sydney Harbour
Blue Line Cruises (tel: 264 3510)
Captain Cook Cruises (tel: 251 5007)
John Cadman (restaurant) (tel: 922 1922)
Matilda Cruises (tel: 264 7377)
Sydney Harbour Explorer (tel: 251 5007)
Tai Pan Cruises (tel: 221 1880)
State Transit Authority Cruises (tel: 29 2622)
Vagabond Cruises (tel: 797 9666)
Pittwater and the Hawkesbury River
Boatshed Cruises (tel: 99 1486)
Lady Hawkesbury (luxury 2 or 4 day cruises) (tel: 27 4548)
Pittwater & Hawkesbury River Cruises (tel: 918 2747)
Riverboat Postman Cruises (tel: 455 1566)
Windsor River Cruises (tel: 621 4154)
Hot air ballooning
Balloon Aloft (tel: 607 2255)

Scuba diving — a popular sport

alloon Flights Australia (tel: 818
599)
alloon Sunrise (tel: 818 1920)
**ature study and Aboriginal
ites.** These trips take you out
to the bush to view wildlife,
ative plants and trees, and
boriginal carvings and other
ites:
ush Picnics (tel: 810 4518)
ush Tucker Tours (tel: 816
381)
eoff Sainty Nature Tours (tel:
32 2661)
Vildlife Study Tours (tel: 457
753)
our guide services. For
ersonalised tours of Sydney:
aureen Fry Guided Tours (tel:
50 7157)
our Hosts (tel: 27 9502)
Valking tours
almain Walking Tours (tel: 818
954)
arling Harbour Guided Walks
el: 327 8887)
mma's Walking Tours of Kings
ross (tel: 356 3413)
arbour City Guides &
ospitality (tel: 27 7183)
arbourside Sydney in a Day
el: 27 4416)
eritage Tours of Hunters Hill
el: 816 4922)
aureen Fry Guided Tours (tel:
50 7157)
he Rocks Walking Tours (tel:
7 6678)
ydney Footnotes (tel: 646 3119)
Valking tours are also
onducted in the Royal Botanic
ardens (tel: 231 8125).

HE SPORTING LIFE

articipation Sports
iving: Courses and ocean
ives can be arranged through
e following operators, who
so hire out diving equipment.

Dive 2000, 2 Military Road,
Neutral Bay (tel: 953 7783)
Pro-Dive, 27 Alfreda Street,
Coogee (tel: 665 6333).
Golf: The Sydney region has
over 80 golf courses, many of
which are open to visitors by
arrangement, while the
following are available to
anyone:
Bondi Golf Course, 5 Military
Road, North Bondi (tel: 30 3170)
Lane Cove Golf Course, River
Road, Northwood (tel: 427 6631)
Moore Park Golf Course, corner
Cleveland Street and Anzac
Parade, Moore Park (tel: 663
1064).
Jogging and running: The
Sydney jogger heads towards
open spaces such as Bondi
Beach, Centennial Park, The
Domain and Manly Beach. If
you're around in August, join
30,000 other running fans in the
annual City to Surf fun run, from
Town Hall to Bondi Beach.
Sailboarding and Sailing:
Sydney Harbour is a good place
to practise your sailing or
sailboarding skills, or try the
popular learner's venue of
Narrabeen Lakes. Instruction is
given by the following
operators, and equipment is
also available for hire.
Australian Sailing School, The
Spit, Mosman (tel: 960 3077)
Klaus' Windsurfing and Sailing
School, 11 Narrabeen Street,
Narrabeen (tel: 913 1765)
Rose Bay Windsurfer School, 1
Vickery Avenue, Rose Bay (tel:
371 7036).
Squash: Squash courts can be
found in most suburbs — check
the yellow pages telephone
directory.
Surfing: The main surfing

beaches along Sydney's coastline all offer, depending on weather conditions, good to excellent surfing conditions. Equipment may be hired at many of the beaches.

Tennis: Tennis is extremely popular in Sydney and the good climate means that the sport is played in both summer and winter, day and night — when many courts are floodlit. Some of the most central courts are: Cooper Park, off Suttie Road, Double Bay (tel: 389 9259) Moore Park Tennis Courts, corner Lang Road and Anzac Parade, Moore Park (tel: 662 7005)
The Palms Tennis Centre, Trumper Park, off Quarry Road, Paddington (tel: 32 4955).

Spectator Sports

Check the sports pages in the *Sydney Morning Herald* for details of current sporting events, or call the Tourist Information Service on 669 5111.
Cricket: The season runs from October to March with major test matches played at the famous Sydney Cricket Ground at Moore Park. Play may be during both day and evening (floodlit) and at weekends.
Football: To Sydneysiders, football means Rugby League, but the three other codes — soccer, Rugby Union and Australian Rules — are all played during the winter season, April to September. The city's main rugby league ground is on Moore Park Road, Paddington.
Greyhound Racing is held at Wentworth Park, Glebe, on most Monday and Saturday

evenings throughout the year.
Horse Racing is a national obsession, mainly because Australians love to gamble. Sydney's four race courses — Randwick, Rosehill, Canterbury and Warwick Farm — rotate meetings on Wednesdays and Saturdays throughout the year. Trotting races are held at Harold Park Paceway, Glebe, on Tuesday and Friday nights.
Motor Racing: Oran Park, near Liverpool, and Amaroo Park, on the way to Windsor, are the city's main motor racing venues. Race meetings are usually held on Sundays through the year.
Sailing: Sydney Harbour's famous and exciting 18 footers race on Saturdays and Sundays from September to April. Spectator ferries leave from Circular Quay. If you are in Sydney at Christmas time, you should not miss the start of the annual Sydney to Hobart yacht race, when the harbour is packed with yachts, ferries and spectator craft.
Surfing: the quintessential Sydney sport! Surf carnivals take place during the summer (October to March) at most of the major surf beaches, and consist of board riding, swimming and surf boat races. Details can be obtained from the Surf Life Saving Association (tel: 597 5588).
Tennis: The Australian tennis season runs from October to February, with the NSW Open, the city's major event, being held at White City in January. Indoor tournaments are held at the Sydney Entertainment Centre at Darling Harbour.

This could be one of the first glimpses you get of Sydney as you land at the Airport; in fact it is one view from the top of Sydney Tower

DIRECTORY

Arriving

Over 20 international airlines service Australia regularly, with flights from the UK, Europe, Asia, North America and the Pacific. Sydney's Kingsford Smith Airport can become very congested at peak times, so be prepared for a fairly slow arrival process. You must clear immigration formalities before collecting your baggage; trolleys are provided free of charge. Customs and quarantine laws are strict and, depending on your embarkation point, a baggage search may be required. The arrival hall, after customs, contains a bank, car hire desks and a travellers' information service. Note also that there is an inbound duty free shop, located before the immigration area.

Transport to the City

Sydney's airport is located 7½ miles (12km) from the city centre. There are several ways to get to your hotel. A taxi rank is located outside the arrival terminal; a cab to the city will cost approximately $A15. The Kingsford Smith Airport bus will, for a small charge, drop you off at any central city hotel. The Airport Express service (yellow and green bus, number 300) runs between the international and domestic air terminals and to the city centre. The ride takes 30 minutes and costs A$3.

Camping

Camping is not permitted anywhere within the inner city

and suburbs. Three caravan and camping sites within reasonable distance of the city are Sundowner North Ryde (9 miles/14km, tel: 88 1933), Ramsgate Beach Caravan Park (10 miles/16km, tel: 529 7329), and Sheralee Tourist Caravan Park (9 miles/14km, tel: 599 7161). Many of the region's national parks permit camping. Contact the National Parks and Wildlife Association (tel: 237 6500) for details of locations and regulations.

Car Breakdown (see Motoring)

Car Hire
Main car hire companies are:
Avis (tel: 516 2877)
Budget (tel: 339 8811)
Hertz (tel: (008) 33 3377) (toll-free)
Letz (tel: 331 3099)
National Car Rental (tel: 332 1233)
Thrifty (tel: 357 5399)
Dollar (tel: 332 1033)
ABC (tel: 357 7700)
For longer distance travel, campervans, motorhomes and four-wheel drive vehicles are readily available:
Australian Outback Four Wheel Drive Hire Co (tel: 211 1270)
Allterrain Rentals (tel: 693 2420)
Brits Rentals (tel: (008) 33 1454) (toll-free)
Budget (tel: 339 8811)
Newmans Campervans (tel: 797 6133)

Chauffeur Driven Services
For a chauffeur driven Rolls Royce, Mercedes or stretch limousine, contact:
Ace Vintage Rentals (vintage and classic cars, tel: 327 4788);
Astra Chauffeured Limousines (tel: 699 2233); Hughes

Chauffeured Limousines (tel: 550 3477); Prestige Limousines (tel: 438 2933).
For a chauffeur driven service with a difference − a horse-drawn taxi − contact The Horse and Carriage Co of Sydney (tel: 27 3181).

Chemist (see **Pharmacy**)

Consulates
All of the major embassies are located in the nation's capital, Canberra, but Sydney has consular representation for most countries.
Canada: AMP Centre, 50 Bridge Street (tel: 231 6522)
UK: Goldfields House, 1 Alfred Street, Circular Quay (tel: 27 7521)
USA: Hyde Park Tower, corner Park and Elizabeth Sts. (tel: 261 9200)

Crime
Overall, Sydney is a very safe city to visit and crime certainly does not reach the levels of bigger cities such as London and New York. However, common sense should always prevail − do not walk in dimly lit areas, such as parks, at night, and always keep a close watch on handbags, wallets and other personal belongings. If you have anything stolen, report it to your hotel and/or the police as soon as possible.

Customs Regulations
All visitors (except New Zealand passport holders) require both a valid passport and visa to enter Australia, as well as an onward ticket and evidence of sufficient funds for the duration of the visit.
Duty free allowances for visitors

The beautiful stained glass windows of the renovated QVB

aged 18 years and over are 250 cigarettes or 250 grams of tobacco; one litre of alcohol and other dutiable goods to a A$400 limit. There is no duty on personal belongings for use during your stay. There is no limit on the amount of personal funds which visitors may bring into Australia.

Quarantine regulations are very strict: Australia is free of many plant diseases and other pests and the importation of fresh or packaged food, fruit, vegetables, seeds, animals and plants or their products is under tight control. On arrival at Sydney airport, the interior of your aircraft will be sprayed with an insecticide, and you must fill out all the customs and quarantine questions on the arrival form which is handed out on the aircraft. Note also that the importation of ivory and the products of other endangered species is not allowed, and the penalties for drug importation offences are very heavy.

Departure Information

On leaving Australia a departure tax of A$10 per person is payable by everyone over 12 years of age. These tax stamps may be purchased from any post office, or at the international air terminal immediately prior to departure. The stamp is affixed to the front of your airline ticket and checked on departure.

Disabled Facilities

Information on facilities for the disabled traveller are available from:
Australia Council for Rehabilitation of the Disabled (ACROD) (tel: (062) 82 4333). In Sydney you can call the Advisory Service for the Handicapped (tel: 918 9770).

Domestic Travel

Airlines
Air New South Wales (tel: 268 1242)
Ansett Airlines (tel: 268 1111)
Australian Airlines (tel: 693 3333)
East-West Airlines (tel: 268 1166)

Coach Services
Ansett Pioneer (tel: 268 1331)
Deluxe Coachlines (tel: 212 4888)
Greyhound Australia (tel: 268 1414)
All services of public transport in Sydney are detailed in State Transit Authority maps, available from most newsagents, or the STA Travel and Tours Centre at 11-31 York Street (tel: 262 3434). Free timetables and travel information are also available here. For timetable information on all urban public transport – bus, rail and ferry services – you can also phone the Metrotrips Service (tel: 954 4422), open from 06.00-22.00hrs daily.

A jungle of concrete skyscrapers makes for a dramatic city skyline on the banks of the Yarra River in Sydney

Buses
Virtually all bus services are operated by the STA, with major terminals at Circular Quay, Wynyard (for north shore buses) and Central Railway Station. Bus routes run along the major city streets to all suburbs. Tickets are purchased from the bus driver, or, at peak times, from ticket sellers at the main city stops. Ring the bell to stop the bus, especially outside the main city area, as it won't necessarily halt at every stop. Apart from special services, Sydney buses are mostly blue and white in colour.
Bus Number 777 is a free city service, operating during business hours on Monday to Friday. It runs in a circular route around the city and is primarily for shoppers. Bus 666 is another

ree service which operates between Hunter Street (near Wynyard Station) and the Art Gallery, and runs at 30 minute intervals daily. For tourists, the red Sydney Explorer bus is the best way to get around the city, while seeing the sights at the same time. It runs on an 11 mile (18km), 20 stop continuous loop from Circular Quay to Kings Cross, Central Railway, the city centre and The Rocks, between 9.30 and 17.00hrs daily. The driver provides a commentary, and you may leave and board the bus at any of its stops during the course of one day. Tickets can be purchased from the bus driver or bought in advance from the Travel Centre of NSW, corner of Pitt and Spring Streets, or the State Transit Authority of NSW Travel Centre at 11-31 York Street.

Trains

Sydney's electric double-decker trains offer the most efficient means of getting around, especially for travel to the suburbs. The city does not have an underground system as such, apart from the city circle line and parts of the Eastern Suburbs railway to Bondi Junction. Suburban trains, which travel to the city's outermost limits, link up with a city circle line which includes Central Station — the city's main suburban and country terminal - Town Hall, Wynyard, Circular Quay, St James and Museum. There is an additional city station at Martin Place. The larger stations have plans of the rail network, which works on a colour-coded line system. Maps are available from stations, or the STA Travel Centre.

Ferries

All ferry services to the north shore and to suburbs west of the bridge such as Balmain, Birkenhead Point and Woolwich depart from Circular Quay. The long run to Manly is covered by both ferries and hydrofoils. All trips afford excellent views of the harbour and city skyline and are a good and economical way to see Sydney from sea level. All tickets are purchased from the Circular Quay ticket booths. Sydney's other waterways such as Pittwater operate their own ferry services.

Monorail

The city's newest, ugliest and most controversial transport system is the monorail, which runs from Darling Harbour to the city, via stations in the Chinatown area, Liverpool Street, Pitt Street and across Pyrmont Bridge. It's really only of use if you're visiting Darling Harbour, or would like to try a ride for its novelty value.

Tickets

Metroten: special tickets which allow ten bus trips for the price of eight.
Day Rover Tickets: unlimited one day use of bus, ferry and train services for A$7.
Sydneypass: this 5 day ticket costs A$25 and gives unlimited travel on bus or ferry services. For overseas visitors only.

Taxis

Except during heavy rain, finding a taxi in Sydney is not a problem. You can either simply hail one on the busier streets,

DIRECTORY

wait at a cab rank — for example, at Circular Quay, Kings Cross, outside railway stations or near Town Hall — or call a taxi service. Cabs are generally white and have a 'For Hire' or 'Not for Hire' sign on the roof, whichever is applicable. Fares are not overly expensive but additional charges are made for waiting time or large amounts of luggage. One drawback is that many Sydney cab drivers are migrants who either do not speak English fluently, or who are not adequately familiar with the intricacies of city streets. It all makes a cab ride more interesting! You are not expected to tip drivers other than perhaps rounding up the fare to the nearest dollar, or unless they are particularly helpful.

ABC Taxis (tel: 922 2233)
Combined Services (tel: 332 8888)
Legion Cabs (tel: 20918)
RSL (tel: 699 0144)

Water Taxis

Sydney offers taxi rides with a difference for those needing to travel across the harbour out of peak times, or to unscheduled destinations. Water taxis will pick you up at any wharf or easy access point on the harbour: rates are expensive.

Aqua Cab (tel: 922 2322 or 929 0477)
Taxis Afloat (tel: 922 4252)

Electricity

Australia's electric current is 240-250 volts AC. While most hotels provide outlets of 110 volt current for shavers and other small appliances, a flat three pin adaptor will be required for most overseas appliances.

Emergency Telephone Numbers

Ambulance (tel: 000)
Fire Brigade (tel: 000)
Police (tel: 000)
Crisis Centre (24 hours) (tel: 358 6577)
Life Line Centre (tel: 264 2222)
Sydney Hospital (tel: 228 2111)
St Vincents Hospital, Darlinghurst (tel: 339 1111/361 2520)
Dental Emergency Information (tel: 267 5919/211 1011)
Chemist Emergency Prescription Service (tel: 438 3333)

Health

Regulations. Unless you are arriving in Australia from tropical regions, no vaccinations are required. If arriving directly from yellow fever, cholera or typhoid infected areas, evidence of inoculations must be provided.

Healthcare. Australian healthcare standards are very high, among the world's best. If you do get sick, pharmacies sell many unrestricted drugs over the counter, or there are plenty of medical centres where you do not need an appointment to see a doctor — ask your hotel for suggestions. British passport holders are entitled to basic medical and public hospital treatment under the Australian government Medicare scheme, but otherwise medical services are quite expensive. You are strongly advised to take out a travel insurance policy which covers medical treatment for

he duration of your stay.
Visitors are permitted to bring
up to four weeks' supply of
prescribed medications. For
larger quantities you should
bring a doctor's certificate for
Customs inspection.

Hire Facilities

Cars (see **Car Hire**)

Boats. Charters of houseboats,
motor cruisers or yachts can be
made through a large number of
operators. Contact the Travel
Centre of NSW (tel: 231 4444)
or full details.

Bicycles. Sydney's traffic makes
city cycling a hazardous
occupation, but it's a pleasant
way to see some of the suburbs.
Australian Cycle Co (tel: 399
1475) and Centennial Park
Cycles (tel: 398 5027).

Camping Equipment. Two of the
largest camping hire operators
are:
Paddy Pallin, 507 Kent Street,

City (tel: 264 2685) and Southern
Cross Equipment, 493 Kent
Street, City (tel: 261 3435).

Horses. Centennial Park is a
great place for a horseback
riding stint. Horses are available
for hire within the Park (tel: 332
2770 or 33 3859 for details).

Holidays — Public and School

Australian public holidays:
New Year's Day Holiday:
1 January
Australia Day: 26 January
Good Friday: March/April
Easter Saturday: March/April
Easter Monday: March/April
Anzac Day: 25 April
Queen's Birthday Holiday: June
— second Monday
Bank Holiday (banks only):
August — first Monday
Labour Day Holiday (NSW):
October — first Monday
Christmas Day: 25 December
Boxing Day: 26 December
On public holidays, all banks,
government departments, post
offices, private offices and most
stores are closed. Public

*A mounted policeman. As a rule
policemen are helpful and polite*

transport is operated on a
limited Sunday-type service.

NSW school holidays:
Summer: mid December to mid
January
Easter: 10 days in March/April
Winter: last week in June and
first week in July
Spring: last week in September
and first week in October

Lost Property
Sydney does not have a central
lost property office. If you lose
something it is best to check
with the local police station. The
Urban Transit Authority has a
lost property office for items left
on buses, trains or ferries (tel:
211 4535). For luggage left in
taxis, call the office of that
particular cab company.

Media
Newspapers and magazines.
The Sydney Morning Herald is
the city's best daily newspaper

*The Australian dollar is the unit of
currency: it is divided into 100 cents*

and is particularly useful on
Mondays for its TV Guide, and
Fridays for the blue Metro
entertainment guide. The *Daily
Mirror* is the afternoon paper,
while Sunday brings the tabloid
style *Sunday Telegraph* and the
Sun Herald. *The Australian* is
the major national daily
newspaper.
Australians have an avid
appetite for magazines and
there are dozens to suit all
tastes on the newsagents'
stands. One publication of
particular interest to the tourist
is the monthly *City Life*
magazine which lists
entertainment venues of all
types.
Radio. Sydney has a very good
range of radio stations covering
news, current affairs, classical
music, chat shows, multi-cultural
programmes and a very wide
variety of popular music. *The
Sydney Morning Herald*
Monday guide gives details of
all programmes for the coming
week.

elevision. Three commercial tations (7, 9 and 10) offer news, oap operas and all the normal 'V fare. The Australian Broadcasting Commission's (ABC) channel 2 is commercial ree and offers a generally better standard, while SBS (Special Broadcasting Service) on Channel 0-28 is the one to watch if you're interested in world news and sport, top quality international films and ethnic programmes. It is also commercial-free. Many pubs and hotels now have Sky channel which focuses mainly on sport and some popular music.

Money Matters

Currency. Australia has a decimal currency system with 100 cents equalling a dollar. The distinctive, brightly coloured notes come in A$5, A$10, A$20, A$50 and A$100 denominations, while coins are 1 cent, 2 cents, 5 cents, 10 cents, 20 cents, 50 cents, A$1 and A$2.

Money Exchange. Most foreign currencies can be exchanged at the airport bank on arrival (outside immigration and customs areas). Otherwise, change money at major city banks, some large stores, or at your hotel. *Bureau de change* offices are operated by American Express and Thomas Cook (useful at weekends) in addition to the normal banking houses. Most major varieties of travellers' cheques are widely accepted.

Exchange Rates. As exchange rates are subject to considerable fluctuation, you should check the Australian

Dollar rate against your own currency before departure.

Credit Cards are widely accepted throughout Sydney and can be used in most hotels and larger restaurants. The most well-known are: American Express, Bankcard, Diners Club, Mastercard and Visa.

American Express (tel: 886 0666)
Diners Club (tel: 236 8923)
Visa Card (tel: 643 1131).

Motoring

Petrol. Petrol or gas is sold by the litre and comes in regular and super grades. Prices vary, but a litre should cost approximately 50 to 60 cents.

Regulations. The first thing to remember is to drive on the left and overtake on the right. It should also be noted that Australians are far from being the world's best drivers and are noted for their aggressiveness. The road death toll, particularly in New South Wales, is horrific, so take care. Traffic congestion can be very bad in Sydney's city centre and on main arterial roads such as the Harbour Bridge crossing and on the westbound Parramatta Road. City parking is also a problem – it is best to travel by public transport around the inner city area. Speed limits vary from 38mph (60kph) in metropolitan areas to 50, 62, or 69mph (80, 100 or 110kph) on other roads and freeways. A list of all road signs and regulations is contained in the *NSW Motor Traffic Handbook,* available from the National Roads and Motorists Association (NRMA), 151 Clarence Street (tel: 260 9122).

Darling Harbour — in something like five years transformed from a rundown eyesore to a fashionable and popular area

Seat belts. It is compulsory to wear seat belts — and this applies to the driver and both front and rear seat passengers. Breaking this law can incur fines. Drink driving laws are also very strict and random breath-testing units are a common sight on both city and country roads.

Breakdowns. The NRMA (address above) is NSW's official motoring association, and in addition to its normal tour planning, road map and information facilities, the NRMA provides a 24-hour emergency breakdown service. Members of most international motoring associations are entitled to receive reciprocal service arrangements with the NRMA. Their emergency service number is 632 0500.

Opening Times

Banks. All banks are closed on Saturday and Sunday. Opening hours are generally from 09.30-16.00hrs Monday to Thursday, and 09.30-17.00hrs on Fridays.

Museums and galleries. Generally 10.00-17.00hrs daily, but check with individual museums as there are several variations, and some close on one day of each week.

Post offices. Monday to Friday, 09.00-17.00hrs.

Shops. Most shops and stores have the following hours: Monday to Friday 09.00-17.30hrs (Thursdays until 21.00hrs); Saturday 09.00-16.00hrs. Some large stores such as Grace Brothers are also open on Sundays. Local suburban corner shops are often open from 08.00-20.00hrs, seven days a week.

Personal Safety

Australia has numerous dangerous and poisonous creatures, such as spiders, scorpions, marine stingers and sharks, but you are most unlikely to come into contact with any of these in Sydney, with the possible exception of marine stingers in the water during summer. If necessary, beaches are closed and warnings given on the radio. Shark attacks off beaches are almost unheard of in Sydney

ese days, due to beach patrols
nd shark-proof nets.
Mosquitoes, flies, biting ants
nd sandflies are all prevalent
n summer and can give
npleasant bites. Protect
ourself with an insect repellent.
unburn can also be a problem,
s the Sydney sun is fierce.
unscreens of varying strengths
re available — be sure to use
hem!
ap water is safe to drink.

Pharmacies
f you need an after-hours
prescription, the 24-hour
Chemist Emergency
Prescription Service (tel: 438
333) can help. In addition, the
ollowing pharmacies are open
fter normal hours:
Blakes Pharmacy, 28b
Darlinghurst Road, Kings Cross
09.00-24.00hrs, every day)
Crest Hotel Pharmacy, 111
Darlinghurst Road, Kings Cross
08.30-24.00hrs, every day)
Serafim Chemist, 389 Bourke
Street, Darlinghurst (24 hours,
every day)
Serafim Chemist, 181 Oxford
Street, Darlinghurst (24 hours,
every day).

Photography
Both print and slide film is
readily available in all major
brands and is not overly
expensive. Prints can be
developed in one to two hours
at many photo shops, while
slides will take at least two to
three days. The Kodak Shop at
333 George Street (tel: 29 8228)
offers a fast slide processing
service for Kodak or other film.

Police
In an emergency, phone 000.

Otherwise, in the case of theft or
any other difficulty, call in at
your nearest police station, or
phone 20966 (the NSW Police
general enquiries number).
Sydney's police are
distinguished by their dark and
pale blue uniforms, and a
peaked, flat topped dark blue
cap.

Places of Worship
The major places of worship are
as follows:
Anglican: St Andrew's
Cathedral, George Street
Baptist: Central Baptist Church,
619 George Street
Roman Catholic: St Mary's
Cathedral, College Street
Interdenominational: Wayside
Chapel, 29 Hughes Street, Kings
Cross
Jewish: The Great Synagogue,
189 Elizabeth Street
Presbyterian: Scots Church, 44
Margaret Street
Uniting: St Stephen's Church,
Macquarie Street

Post Office
Post offices are located in most
suburbs and around the city
centre, with the General Post
Office (GPO) at Martin Place.
All post offices provide the
normal services — stamps,
aerogrammes, telegrams etc,
and larger offices also have
Electronic Post facilities, which
include facsimiles, telexes and
lettergrams. If you need to send
an urgent message, do so
through your hotel or from the
GPO telegram office on King
Street, which is open 24 hours a
day. Stamps are available from
hotels and some tourist shops
which sell postcards. Sydney
post boxes are red.

Student and Youth Travel

There are few concessions for overseas students in Sydney; local students get reductions on cinema and theatre tickets, and also on public transport, but this does not apply to people from overseas. It is always worth bringing an international student card, however, and attempting to get concessions.

Telephones

Public telephones are located at post offices, public buildings and in phone booths throughout the city. Local calls currently cost 30 cents (20 and 10 cent pieces) for an unlimited time. Some public telephones are specifically for long distance and international calls and major hotels now have a credit card payphone system. Calling from your hotel room phone is easier, but generally more expensive for long distance calls.

The area code for Sydney is 02

Ticket Agencies

Sydney's main ticket booking service for all major events such as opera, ballet, theatre, sport c rock concerts is Ticketek (tel: 266 4800), which operates on a credit card paying system. Alternatively, they will advise where your nearest Ticketek office is located. The Halftix booth at Martin Place, near Elizabeth Street, sells half price tickets from 12 noon to 20.00hrs on the day of performance (Monday to Saturday only) for a major performances. Cinema tickets must be bought at individual theatres.

Time

Sydney is on Eastern Standard

Remember: the water may look lovely and inviting, but heed warnin signs and follow the lifeguards' instructions when swimming

ime, which is 10 hours ahead
f GMT. From October to March
summer) Sydney has one hour
f daylight saving, where the
locks are put forward one hour
e: 11 hours ahead of GMT).
Within Australia, Sydney is half
n hour ahead of Adelaide and
Darwin (Central Standard
'ime), and 2 hours ahead of
'erth (Western Standard Time).

'ipping
Generally, Australians do not
p, except for particularly good
ervice, and with the following
xceptions. In restaurants
ervice is not normally added to
ne bill, so a 10 per cent tip is
ustomary, but not obligatory,
or good service. Taxi fares are
ften rounded up to the nearest
lollar as a tip for the driver, and
t is common practice to leave
mall change on the bar in pubs
or hotels for the bartender. The
ipping of hotel porters etc. is at
your discretion and is optional.

Toilets
Public toilets are located at
ailway and bus stations, in
parks and public places and the
arge department stores. They
are generally clean and
well-maintained with adequate
supplies of toilet paper, and are
ree. If you can't find a public
oilet and are really desperate,
pop into one of the city's many
pubs and use theirs.

Tourist Information
The Travel Centre of New South
Wales, 16 Spring Street (tel: 231
4444) is open from 09.00-
17.00hrs Monday to Friday, and
is the chief Sydney information
and booking agency for
accommodation, tours and
travel. (Write to GPO Box 11,
Sydney, NSW 2000.)
Tourist Information Service (tel:
669 5111)
Travellers Information Service
(Airport) (tel: 669 1583)
Rocks Visitors Centre (tel: 27
4972)
Tourist Newsfront (tel: 27 7197)
National Parks & Wildlife
Service (tel: 585 6333)
Manly Tourist Promotions (tel:
977 1088)
Parramatta Tourist Information
Centre (tel: 630 3703)
In addition, tourist information
booths are located at Circular
Quay, Pitt Street Mall (between
King and Market Streets), at the
top of Sydney Tower, and on
Martin Place (near Elizabeth
Street).

Tourist Offices — Overseas
The Australian Tourist
Commission offices in the UK,
USA and Canada can provide
advance information on Sydney
or any other part of Australia:

UK
London: Gemini House, 10-18
Putney Hill, London SW18 6AA
(tel: (01) 780 1496)

USA
New York: 31st Floor, 489 Fifth
Avenue, New York, NY 10017
(tel: (212) 687 6300)
Los Angeles: Suite 1200, 2121
Avenue of the Stars, Los
Angeles, CA 90067 (tel: (213)
552 1988)
Chicago: 150 North Michigan
Avenue, Suite 218, Chicago, ILL
60601 (tel: (312) 781 5150)

Canada
Toronto: Suite 1730, 2 Bloor
Street West, Toronto, Ontario
M4W 3E2 (tel: (416) 925 9575)

LANGUAGE

Although it is a widely held belief that Australians speak English, any visitor will soon become aware that not only is the accent sometimes difficult to understand, but that there are many subtle differences in the use of words. Australians speak 'Strine', an informal, even lazy, form of slang which may often be ungrammatical, but is certainly colourful and inventive. Many words, and even names, are abbreviated and familiarised — thus John becomes 'Johnno', Paddington becomes 'Paddo' and 'garbo' is easier to say than garbage

collector. Unlike the USA, where many ethnic words have passed into common usage, courtesy of the Jewish, Irish or Italian communities, Australia has not absorbed many words or expressions from its multicultural communities. It is common, however, to hear languages such as Greek, Italian, Japanese, Vietnamese, Turkish or Cantonese spoken on the street. Aboriginal languages are more likely to be heard in the outback, but several Aboriginal words have left their mark on often tongue-twisting

All Sydney's beaches are patrolled by the Surf Life Saving Association

lace names.

he following glossary lists
ome commonly used Australian
xpressions.

bo Aborigine (impolite)

rvo afternoon

ack of beyond the outback

arbie barbecue

attler a person who struggles
  hard

eaut very good, great

loke man

ludger a sponger, user or lazy
  person

ottle shop off licence

uckley's chance no or little hope

ush countryside (implies
  unspoilt)

hook chicken

huck throw

orroboree Aboriginal
  ceremonial gathering

rook sick or no good

ag/daggy dreadful, as in
  unfashionable

aks trousers

amper unleavened bread (bush
  food)

ero derelict (generally
  drunkard)

ill idiot

inky di the real thing

unny toilet

air dinkum the real thing,
  genuine

ooty football

'day hello (universal greeting)

alah fool (after the parrot)

arbo garbage collector

ive it the flick get rid of it

rizzle complain

rog alcohol of any sort

oon yobbo, loudmouth

ourno journalist

iwi New Zealander

air, Larrikin unruly or irreverent
  person

ob up arrive

urk a racket or illegal scheme

Mate best friend, or merely a form
  of address to someone
  unknown

Middy 10-ounce beer glass

Mozzie mosquito

OS overseas

Ocker the classic Aussie
  beer-drinking loudmouth
  (usually male)

Oz Australia

Perve to admire a member of the
  opposite sex

Plonk cheap wine

Pokie slot or fruit machine

Pom, Pommie English person

Postie mailman

Ratbag offbeat or somewhat
  dubious person

Ripper good

Salvo Salvation Army member

Sandshoes sneakers

Schooner large beer glass

She'll be right it'll all be OK

Shoot through to leave

Shout a round of drinks

Snags sausages

Spunky good looking, sexy

Station large farm, ranch

Stubby small bottle of beer

Stubbies working men's shorts

Ta thank you

Ta ta goodbye

Togs swimming costume

Truck lorry

Tucker food

Uni university

Ute utility, pick-up truck

Vegemite spread, similar to
  Marmite

Walkabout from the Aboriginal
  habit of walking long
  distances, also 'gone
  walkabout' as in not with it

Whinge complain

Wimp spineless person

Wowser killjoy

Yakka work

Yarn chat or conversation

Yobbo loudmouth, unruly person

INDEX/ACKNOWLEDGEMENTS

The Automobile Association would like to thank the following photographers and libraries for their assistance in the compilation of this book.

ANNE MATTHEWS 31 Hyde Park Barracks, 50 Blue Mountains, 70 Phillip's Foote restaurant, 76 Country pub, 113 Queen Victoria Building, 120 Darling Harbour.

J BORTHWICK 95 Darling Harbour, 96 Eastside, 97 Nightclub.

CHRISTINE OSBORNE PICTURES 16 Woolloomooloo, 47 Windsurfing, 49 Joggers, 69 Sautéed eel, 73 Italian restaurant, 75 Doyles, 80/1 Paddington Market, 85 Apartments, 86 Inter-Continental Hotel, 89 Backpackers, 99 Sydney suburbs, 102/3 Children at play, 108 Scuba school, 117 Rush hour, 118 Currency, 124 Lifeguard.

MARY EVANS PICTURE LIBRARY 7 Captain Cook, 9 Sydney cove.

NATURE PHOTOGRAPHERS LTD 57 Cockatoo (D Hutton), 58 Giant petrel (E Lemon), 60 Banksia (K J Carlson), 63 Wallaby (C B Carver), 64 Kookaburra, 65 Lorikeet (R S Daniell), 67 Koala bear (T D Schilling), 105 Wombat (H Clark).

SPECTRUM COLOUR LIBRARY 10 Firing salute, 19 Circular Quay East, 24/5 The Rocks, 29 The Observatory, 32/3 Royal Botanic Gardens, 35 Hyde Park, 36 Queen Victoria Building, 38 Darling Harbour, 41 Elizabeth Bay House, 45 Vaucluse House, 53 Canberra, 55 Fitzroy Falls, 61 Royal National Park, 79 Queen Victoria Building, 83 Martin Place, 91 Kings Cross, 92 Opera House, 101 Royal Easter Show, 111 View to Heads, 114 Skyline, 122 Danger.

ZEFA PICTURE LIBRARY (UK) LTD Cover Opera House, 4 Sydney, 13 Aerial Sydney, 14 Business area, 21 Harbour bridge, 42 Paddington House, 107 Watsons Bay.